This book is dedicated to my family, especially my mother, Virginia Goren. Your love, support, and encouragement have allowed me to fulfill my dreams. Thank you for always being there for me.

The
BUSINESSWOMAN'S HANDBOOK

Practical Tips for Moving Up
the Corporate Ladder

Roseann Harrington, M.B.A.

ISBN 978-0615616995

Printed in the United States of America

Book and jacket design by William Gridley

First Edition

CONTENTS

PREFACE

CHAPTER 1 • PAGE 1
Let's Get Started

Don't Count Your Chickens Before They're Hatched
Location, Location, Location
Think Before You Jump

CHAPTER 2 • PAGE 7
Finding the Right Career

Find Something That Fits
Determine What You Want Your Future to Look Like
Find a Company, Industry or Profession
Assessing Yourself

CHAPTER 3 • PAGE 13
Applying for a Job or Promotion

CHAPTER 4 • PAGE 20
Establishing Yourself in a New Job or Work Team

Common Challenges Faced
How to Find a Mentor

CHAPTER 5 • PAGE 25
Communicating Effectively

Clarify the Message
Understand Different Communication Styles
DISC Communication Styles
Social Media Do's and Don'ts

CHAPTER 6 • PAGE 34
Bridging the Generational Divide

The Six Living Generations
Words That Drive Supervisors Crazy

CHAPTER 7 • PAGE 46

How to Manage Your Boss

Building Trust
Recognize Your Supervisor's Style
Tips for Managing Your Boss

CHAPTER 8 • PAGE 54

Corporate Etiquette and Professionalism

Acting in a Professional Manner
Business Correspondence
Professional Attire and Grooming
Professional Attire Do's and Don'ts
Types of Attire
The Power of the Pump

CHAPTER 9 • PAGE 65

Representing Your Organization

Tips for When You Attend Business Functions and Meetings
Traveling on Company Business
Proper Place Setting

CHAPTER 10 • PAGE 76

Moving Up the Ranks

The Waiting Game
Tips for Moving Up the Ranks

CHAPTER 11 • PAGE 88

Creating Your Personal Brand

Alignment Between the Truth and Perception
Three Phases in Building a Brand
Steps in Building a Personal Brand

CHAPTER 12 • PAGE 97

Networking and Business Development

How to Start a Conversation
Tips on How to Network
The Benefits of Volunteering
Business Development and Entertaining Tips

CHAPTER 13 • PAGE 106

Business Ethics and Human Resources

Purchasing Goods and Services
Contracts
Dealing with Awkward Comments and Sexual Advances

CHAPTER 14 • PAGE 111

Taking on a Management Role

The Right Leader at the Right Time
Supporting the CEO
The Management Pyramid
Qualities of a Good Manager
Things a Good Leader Should Know How to Do

CHAPTER 15 • PAGE 131

The Value of Experience

Practice Makes Perfect

CHAPTER 16 • PAGE 134

Having Children While Working

Timing Is Everything
Managing Stereotypes and Perceptions
The Generational Divide
Dealing with Working Mother's Guilt
Moving Forward While Raising Children

CHAPTER 17 • PAGE 143

Balancing Work and Family

Establish Reasonable Expectations
Strive for a Balanced Life
Final Words of Wisdom

PAGE 147

About the Author

PREFACE

The inspiration for this book was my desire to pass on the knowledge and experience I gained working my way up through the ranks to other women looking for ways they, too, can succeed in business. I was fortunate to have tremendous mentors throughout my career, and I wanted to share the lessons I have learned with the next generation of female leaders.

By writing about my experiences, I was able to relive the ups and downs and twists and turns that have made me the person I am today. Looking back over my career provided me the opportunity to do things differently and help readers learn from my mistakes. As it's said, "Hindsight is 20/20."

I had always wanted to write a book, but what prompted me to actually sit down and do it was the encouragement of numerous young women I have supervised, mentored, or met over the years. Many of these individuals were looking for advice and tips on how to deal with the trials and tribulations of moving up the corporate ladder.

My hope is that readers will find the tips listed in the book helpful and that it will become a valuable resource throughout their careers.

– Roseann Harrington

CHAPTER 1

Getting Started

My own career had a rocky start and is proof that you can overcome setbacks and still make it to the top. It also illustrates that experiences early in your career can benefit you later in life. Sometimes it seemed as if for every two steps forward there was one step back and that the rungs of the ladder were farther apart than expected, but eventually I made it to the top. It just took perseverance and a good attitude.

I graduated college in 1984 during tough economic times and, like many of you, was a high achiever. My heart was set on working for the company where I had interned during my senior year. The organization had a history of hiring their interns, so I felt pretty good about my employment prospects. Unfortunately, there was a hiring freeze due to restructuring – and I was frozen out. This led to my first lesson learned.

Don't Count Your Chickens Before They're Hatched

I can't tell you how many people I have talked to who have wasted valuable time and effort on a "sure thing" to the exclusion of other opportunities. Whether applying for a new job or a promotion, they were overly confident that they would be selected. In business there is never a "sure thing." It took me a few times to figure this out, but I eventually learned.

Be careful when you are told that you are the perfect person for a job or promotion. There is never certainty when it comes to work, and sometimes you end up with the short straw. Do not leave anything to chance. As long as you feel as if you could not have done anything more, you need to learn from the experience and move on. However, if you had some part in your own demise by not preparing for an interview or being overconfident, you need to learn from your mistakes and not blame others. In a recent interview, a top candidate for a job blew it by not taking the process seriously. She thought she was the most qualified candidate and wasn't worried about the competition. The other candidates gave 150 percent and outshined her. The panel had no choice but to select someone else. Don't let this happen to you.

Having missed out on a sure thing myself, I know how discouraging it can be, and how it can knock you back on your heels. This is especially true if it is a tough job market. Finding myself in a tough job market, I made the knee-jerk decision to move to Miami, Florida, and live with my sister. This led to my second lesson learned.

Location, Location, Location

Not being able to find a job in New Orleans, where I went to college, I found a job working for a plastics manufacturer in Miami. I moved in with my sister and had some friends from college in Miami so I assumed all would work out well. I knew nothing about Miami before making the move and assumed that all cities were alike. What I didn't know at the time was that all cities are not alike. Miami was very different from New Orleans, and the cost of living was much higher.

My suggestion to anyone starting out or looking to relocate is to *spend some time in the city you are considering* and do things you would want to do on the weekends if you were living there full time. If you break the bank in one weekend, you know that you have a problem. It is no fun to be staring at candy in the window and not be able to afford it.

You also need to seriously *consider commute times.* As a supervisor, I have known employees who take a job, and then a year later decide that the commute time and costs associated with it are a hardship.

Look at your lifestyle and determine what you need in a city. If you are miserable outside work, it can negatively impact job satisfaction. I really liked my job in Miami, but it required a long commute in bumper-to-bumper traffic. In fact, due to my limited salary, I had to live in a more remote area and had a long drive to everything. One of the things I liked most about New Orleans was that it was compact and had good mass transit. I overlooked these things in Miami because I was so desperate to find a job.

It is also important to *research the cost of living.* My salary was not enough to support myself and pay off my student loans. I was forced to get a second job working at a department store. I worked 30 hours a week in addition to 40 hours at my day job and had no free time and no money. This was not the lifestyle I wanted to lead. In addition, I missed my family and friends back home in Orlando.

Another thing you need to do is *evaluate the city's crime rate*. Miami, unfortunately, was in the midst of its "Miami Vice" phase and had a number of drug-related, drive-by shootings that often took the lives of several innocent people. In fact, one Saturday morning I was cleaning the house when someone shot a bullet through the sliding glass door of my apartment. I hit the ground, panicked.

To make matters worse, Miami had another menace to deal with – the pillow-case rapist. The rapist was breaking into women's apartments in the area where I lived. I was so scared that when I would come home late at night from my second job, I would run to my apartment. I would immediately call my friend from work, and she would stay on the line while I searched every closet and looked under the beds. I slept with a chair wedged against both the front door and my bedroom door.

I was miserable, to say the least. I had never really thought much about *where* I would work because I was focused on getting a job anywhere. Where you live is extremely important, so do your research before making a decision and avoid knee-jerk reactions.

Think Before You Jump

You need to take the appropriate amount of time to look at all facets of a job before making a decision to accept the position. If not, you could end up worse off than when you started. That is what happened to me. Moving home was the best decision I ever made, but I went about it the wrong way by accepting the first position that came my way. Regretably I did not research the organization. The job offered more money and a short commute. It all sounded so good. As it turned out there was not much good about the job. Sure enough, three months after I was hired, my whole department was laid off, including my boss.

If I found it a humbling experience not finding a job right after college, it was far more humiliating to stand in the unemployment line. The worst part was when they contacted my former employer in Miami to verify my work history. I was so embarrassed when I heard that they were "worried" about me. Ugh!!!

Having talked to a number of women who are unhappy at work and want to leave, I always advise them not to quit. It is easier to find a job when you already have one. Unless you have been laid off or had to relocate to a different city, it is hard to explain why you would leave a good job without saying something negative about your former employer. *(I go into more details about interviewing in Chapter 3.)*

By now, you are probably wondering whether I did anything right. The answer is – yes, I did! Maybe the third time truly is a charm. I learned from my previous mistakes and started to think things through before acting or not acting. I looked at my prior work and experience and set out to find something that had all the positives and none of the negatives. My favorite position was my internship at the phone company. I really liked the corporate environment and that they provided a service. My mother brought me to a few chamber of commerce meetings and business association socials to network. It was at one of those events that I met the head of corporate communications at the Orlando Utilities Commission (OUC). He had a public information coordinator position open, which was similar to what I was doing as an intern at the phone company. I applied the next day and got the job.

When I came home from my first day at work, my mother asked me how it went. I told her that there must be something in the water because they were the nicest group of people I had ever met. Twenty-six years later, I still feel the same. I hope that the tips I provide in this book will help you find a career that is as fulfilling as mine has been.

CHAPTER 2

Finding the Right Career

Find Something That Fits

As a fashion lover, and someone who also is known for devising analogies, I compare finding the right career to shopping for clothes – *find something that fits*.

When selecting a job or career, take time to evaluate your likes and dislikes, strengths and weaknesses. When you find something that is the perfect fit, everything falls into place. When you feel good in a job, it shows. You are more motivated, and that influences your performance. Just like receiving compliments when your outfit looks great, you will get noticed if you are in a job that maximizes your strengths. If you are in a job where your primary responsibility is not a good fit, your performance will suffer or you will experience stress and be unhappy.

As you evaluate careers, match your skills with the job requirements, level of desired socialization, work environment, and what makes you happy. Your goal is to align your abilities with the requirements of the job. The more relevant work experience you have, the quicker you will be able to start making contributions to the team and the less training you will require. It is tough enough trying to understand a new company, but it's even harder if you have to learn the job, too. Don't exaggerate your work experience. I have had employees who talked a good talk and sounded as if they knew more than they did. This is dangerous because your supervisor doesn't know what you don't know.

First and foremost, make sure that you have the basic skills required to perform the job, including education and personality type. Are you really good with numbers? Are you a great writer? Are you organized and detail-oriented? I often have people tell me that they want to be in "management." But everyone in management has to supervise a specific area, and they have to be experts in their area. What seat do you want at the table?

Determine What You Want Your Future to Look Like

No one knows what the future will bring, but we all have dreams. We have a general idea about whether we want a family, like to travel, desire to be involved in the community or our church or strive to continue to grow and learn.

Women, need to take a hard look at what will make them happy in the future. How do you feel about a job that requires you to travel or to work nights and weekend? Do you want to manage people or do you prefer to be a professional and work independently? Do you see yourself as a mid-level manager or as vice president or CEO? These are some of the questions you need to ask yourself.

Take the time early in your career to identify what makes you happy and what doesn't. It will help you focus on the right opportunities and not waste your time in positions that will frustrate you.

It's important when selecting a job that you find something you like to do. You should have at least one task you perform every day that you enjoy to ensure your happiness at work. I love to write and that is something I get to do every single day. If you like what you do for a living, it will show, and you will be more productive. Attitude is extremely important, and it is easier to be positive and enthusiastic if you enjoy what you are doing.

The more you know about yourself, the easier it will be to find a job that is a good fit. Some people need to change jobs frequently because they get bored; others are looking for a long-term opportunity and are willing to move a little slower to gain the expertise required to take on more responsibility.

Find a Company, Industry or Profession

If you want to see how to get to the top, look at the women who are already there. In most cases, you will find women who worked their way up through the ranks at a company or through a specific industry or excelled in a profession such as accounting, public relations, engineering or law. These women focused their efforts and became highly valued experts with extensive work-related experience. In many cases, they continued their education, took lateral moves to enhance their experience, and found other ways to gain a breadth of knowledge necessary to make themselves valued leaders.

Assessing Yourself

Here is your first assignment: Read the section below and then write a detailed, one-paragraph description of yourself.

Answer the following questions:

1) What activity do you think you need to do every day at work? For example, is it writing, analyzing, organizing, working with computers, or being creative?

2) What level of socialization do you need? Is it important to interact with others on a daily basis? If so, do you prefer face-to-face interaction, telephone, Internet, etc.?

3) Do you prefer to work alone or with others? Do you like being part of a team, or would you prefer something that allows you to work more independently, like sales?

4) What type of compensation do you want? Do you want to have a fixed salary that you can count on, or would you like to have part of it based on commissions?

5) What type of work environment do you need? Do you need an organization that is family-friendly and allows flextime, telecommuting, or other options? Some organizations are very corporate and others are more relaxed and allow you to wear jeans. You can't change them, so unless you are willing to

follow the rules, you need to consider these issues before accepting a position.

6) What is your level of commitment? Are you looking to move up through the ranks and work whatever hours are required to gain the experience necessary, or are you looking for a way to earn money? Be honest with yourself.

7) What motivates you most? Is it money, recognition, accomplishment, or an opportunity to learn and grow? Most sales people have to be motivated by money because their compensation is directly tied to their sales.

Now that you have read the questions, begin to write your description. I will get you started by letting you read mine.

I am a high-socialization, accomplishment-oriented person. I need to be around people and have the ability to interact with others on a daily basis. I am very creative and detail-oriented and love to learn new things. I need a position in which I can write, review, or edit on a daily basis. I like a fast-paced work environment and can manage multiple projects at the same time. I like a corporate environment that provides me the opportunity to learn, grow and rise through the ranks. I am willing to sacrifice pay for stability, meaningful work, and a family-friendly environment.

Writing your own personal description will help you focus on what is really important to you. When looking at new positions, compare them to your description. If the job aligns with your needs, it will probably be a good fit. If it doesn't, be careful because you are going against your grain, and you might end up unhappy.

Now that you know a little more about yourself, it is time to talk about finding the right job. These rules apply whether you are interviewing for a new position or posting for an internal promotion.

CHAPTER 3

Applying for a Job or Promotion

Applying for a job is never easy, because it involves selling yourself – and that doesn't come easy to most of us. It's like walking a tightrope. You want to show interest, but not oversell yourself; exude confidence, but not come off as cocky. In most cases, you are nervous, and people react to pressure in different ways. The tips below were developed through personal experience reviewing hundreds of resumes, interviewing dozens of candidates, and hearing input from others who have extensive job interviewing experience. The end result is a list of *Cardinal Rules of Applying for a Job*.

1. **Use proper spelling and grammar.** Most resumes and cover letters are viewed online, and mistakes are highlighted in color. Your documents should not light up like a Christmas tree when viewed by a prospective employer. They will get tossed in the trash can immediately. Use spell check, and then find someone who knows proper grammar to review your cover letter and résumé. In fact, have a few people review the material.

2. **Verify potential employer information.** Inaccurate employer information is a big turnoff. I can't tell you how many times I have received a letter with my name or my title wrong. I've even been called "Mr." This tells me that I would have to

worry about you not getting basic information correct while performing your job. Why would I hire someone who doesn't even take the time to get my name right?

3. **Format your résumé correctly.** Your résumé should be easy to read, with accurate, up-to-date information. Your information will be verified, so never stretch the truth. If you have taken on projects here and there, list them under a general topic like "contract work." When you list projects separately, it looks as if you stayed at numerous places for short periods of time. A prospective employer will think that you jump from position to position or you have a problem getting along with coworkers or supervisors. There are numerous web sites to help you format your résumé. Search "résumé template," and read every thing listed on the page. These sites also include tips on writing content.

4. **Tailor your résumé and cover letter to the job you are pursuing.** With today's technology, there is no excuse for not tailoring your résumé to the job description. I am not a fan of web sites that send your résumé to any organization with a key word like "marketing" in their job description. They might be efficient, but they are not effective. In addition, use proper terminology, avoid acronyms, and don't use abbreviations. For those of you who are just starting your career, don't use slang as it can make you seem "too young" for the position.

5. **Network.** It's difficult for a high achiever to be unemployed, but it is no time to go underground. The more people who know you are looking for a job, the more eyes and ears you have helping you find employment. The majority of people whom I have hired found out about the position from a friend. All it takes is having someone tell a potential employer to look for your résumé. In most cases, they will. This is a big deal when you consider that most positions you may be applying for may generate more than 100 applications.

6. **Stay active.** Don't let yourself become discouraged. Get up at a reasonable hour, eat well, exercise, and make sure you have plenty of social interaction. You do not want to come in for an interview sluggish or appear to lack energy. This is the time in your life when you need to have energy and enthusiasm. I tell people to go and sit in a coffee shop and keep themselves busy with a laptop, book, or papers, because it gives you a place to go where you are around other people. There is a chance that you might run in to someone who knows about a job opportunity.

7. **Volunteer or do contract work.** Volunteering and contract work for either a non-profit or a business is a great way to keep busy and make valuable connections. Offer to intern or work free of charge in order to gain experience in a new area. This is becoming a popular way for employers to get extra

help, and it also allows them to justify the need for a new position. Many employers are also hiring people on a contract basis until they can gain approval for full-time staff. Be open to options like these because they provide an opportunity to get your foot in the door.

8. **Make a good first impression.** Proper attire and professional behavior are essential. Supervisors hate having to talk to someone about inappropriate workplace attire. If the potential employer thinks this will be an issue with you, they will not hire you. The only thing they should remember about your attire is that you looked professional and presentable. Too much jewelry, especially nose and lip rings, can be a turn off. Avoid extremes: don't be overly enthusiastic or too quiet.

9. **Watch your body language.** Employers want someone who understands proper behavior. Make sure that you shake hands (not too hard or too soft) and make eye contact. Poor posture is another no-no. Slouching in your chair, rocking back and forth, or hanging your arms over the back in an overly relaxed fashion are distracting.

10. **Avoid annoying habits.** This includes any habit that makes a noise, such as chewing gum, tapping your nails on the table, biting your nails, or clearing your throat. No one likes to sit in a meeting with people who do these things. Do not bring anything to drink or eat with you to an interview, including coffee or bottled water.

11. **Learn about the company.** Most interviewers will ask you questions about their business. They will assume that you have gone to their web site in advance of your interview. If you don't have time to learn about a potential employer, then save everyone a lot of time and skip the interview.

12. **Do not bash your former employer.** Most potential employers will think that if you speak poorly about your former boss or company, you will do the same about them. Find something positive to say about your last job and focus on the positives. For example: "It was a great learning experience." Under no circumstances should you highlight any past negative situations with a past employer in a cover letter. Secure an interview first, and if the employer asks for details, always explain them as positively as possible.

13. **Practice interviewing.** Potential employers expect interviews to be a two-way street. They expect you to keep them engaged. Present yourself with energy and enthusiasm. Practice with a friend or family member in order to gain confidence in your interviewing skills. Arrive early for the interview. When you are brought in to the room for the interview, introduce yourself and thank the person for meeting with you. Bring a pad and pen. Ask follow-up questions, and be prepared for them to ask you whether you have any questions. Have three questions prepared. For example: What are you looking for in an

employee? What do you feel is the most important skill required to successfully do the job? Are there opportunities for me to learn and grow my talents? What is your management style? (Remember, you need to make sure this is a good fit for you, too.)

14. **Know when to talk and when to listen.** A job interview should be a conversation. Avoid monopolizing the discussion and trying too hard to convince someone you are the best candidate. To avoid the super-salesman syndrome, watch the interviewer for cues on whether he or she is still engaged or not. When I am talking to a super salesman, I tend to stop talking. If you catch yourself in a similar situation, one where the interviewer stops talking or seems uninterested, ask him or her a question and then sit back and listen.

15. **Do not over-talk when asked a tough question.** Sometimes interviewers ask questions that are tough or even awkward. Even though they are not supposed to ask about your personal life, it happens. Remember that interviewing is a two-way street. It is an opportunity to see whether you want to work for the individual or company. One poorly worded question could be considered a mistake, but if it happens more than once, it should send up a red flag. People are on their best behavior during an interview, so if they cross the line there, they may do the same later. Keep your responses simple.

16. **Do not price yourself out of the market.** Salary issues are tough. Most employers will not make offers outside the advertised salary range. If you are not willing to budge on salary, understand that your demands might keep you from being considered for the position. Nowadays, supervisors don't have as much leeway with salary as they once did, especially in a buyer's market, where there are a number of qualified people who are willing to do the job for the posted salary. Employers are getting creative when it comes to compensation. Some will offer extra vacation time in lieu of salary or commit to a certain number of hours of overtime pay.

The most important thing to remember is to be realistic. From salary to titles to tasks, you need to be comfortable with pre-established guidelines. Most importantly, interviewing is not a game or a chance to do a *practice* run, so only apply for positions that really interest you and give it your all. Word gets around, and people talk, especially in smaller cities and within industries. You do not want to be known as someone who is fishing for a promotion.

CHAPTER 4

Establishing Yourself in a New Job or Work Team

Starting a new job is never easy. Sometimes things go well, and you fit right in. Other times, it can be a rocky transition. If you want to improve your chances for making the change successful, take the time up front, if applicable, to learn as much as you can about the people you will be working with and the new company. The more you know about a new job or company, the easier the transition.

Common Challenges Faced

- **When the person you thought you would be working for changes.** This is particularly hard when your new boss is someone you have not met before. It is normal to feel disappointed and concerned, especially if you were not notified before starting work. My advice is to try and remain positive and give the new supervisor a chance. Hopefully, the actual work won't change, and you will get along with your new boss. If the job does change, you need to let the new supervisor know that you took the position based on what was previously offered and discuss your future responsibilities. You might find that you will need to choose whether to play ball or get off the team.

- **Projects you thought you would work on are eliminated.** This often occurs as a result of budget cuts, and there is nothing a supervisor can do. Even though the project was cut, don't take it out on your new boss, who is probably disappointed, too. Go in to the new position with the right attitude, and look for new projects that are just as interesting. Volunteering to take on additional work always gets noticed.

- **You don't click with your coworkers.** You need to have patience and perseverance. It often takes a while to fit in, so don't get discouraged if things aren't great at first. Just like in high school, the worst part of not fitting in is not having a friend at work to go to lunch with or talk to during the day. My advice is to find something to do during lunch, like meeting friends outside your company, working out, doing errands, or reading.

- **You don't get along with your boss.** We are all looking for the perfect boss, but sometimes it doesn't happen. There was probably a time in your life when you had a teacher that you didn't like, and the odds of having this happen at work are just as high. You need to do your best to get along. I had a boss who was a chain smoker, and she and I had to share a glass-enclosed office. Neither of us was happy with this arrangement. After a few months, it became unbearable, so I began to look for alternatives that would make her happy. There was a large,

21

open area on the floor that had two desks, but only one was being used. I asked my boss if we could move my desk in to the space. This arrangement would provide her with the privacy she needed to do her job. She liked the idea, and we sold it to our vice president. Instead of getting bitter, be creative.

How to Find a Good Mentor

I have been fortunate to have a number of good mentors throughout my entire life. I was lucky to have been raised by a mother who was a successful businesswoman and a great mentor. My mother talked to me about her work experiences and it allowed me to gain important insight in to the business world. She also taught me to look for solutions, especially ones that helped you avoid a confrontation.

A perfect example of this scenario was when I began work at OUC. My desk chair broke and I needed a new one. I asked my department vice president for a new chair. At the time, there were hardly any female professionals in the workplace and so my boss was unsure what type of new chair to purchase for me – one with arms or without. You see, secretaries were not allowed to have arms on their chairs; they were only for professionals. However, I was a professional and a woman and so he did not know how to respond. Instead of confronting him, I went to a storage closet and found an old chair with arms and put it at my desk. Problem solved!

The most important thing about finding the right mentor is to look for someone who has both the time and desire to offer you help. Your mentor needs to feel vested in your success if the relationship is going to be beneficial. Mentors can be at your company, people you meet through school or in the community. College professors are great mentors. In fact, you may have many mentors in your life at various points in your career.

I would have never been able to write this book if it were not for the mentoring provided to me by Dr. Greg Marshall, Charles Harwood Professor of Marketing and Strategy at the Rollins College Crummer School of Business. He has me guest lecture in is marketing class each semester and encouraged me to compile my presentations in to a book. In addition, his class provided me an opportunity to meet many of the women I mentored and interviewed as part of the researching of this book.

I met many of my mentees through guest lecturing sessions. At the end of my presentation, I offer to follow-up with students who have questions and provide my business card. I have had a number of female students reach out to me and met with them all. I am still mentoring some of the women and am proud of their accomplishments. Every once in a while we will touch base and they know I am always available to provide advice or just moral support. In addition, the mentoring relationships have benefited me. I have been able to learn from the work my mentees are doing in areas outside of my expertise. It's called "reverse mentoring."

Take advantage of opportunities like the one mentioned above to gain advice from respected business leaders. At a minimum they will be flattered that you were impressed with them enough to want their advice.

Your own organization can be a good place to find a mentor. I have had two young women outside of my area ask to meet with me under the auspices of learning how I got to my position. After our first meeting, they both asked me if we could continue meeting and I gladly agreed. I am now vested in their success and look for ways to advance their careers and help them balance their work and family responsibilities.

I had both male and female mentors throughout my career and both have been wonderful. Do not feel restricted by the gender of the person whom you ask for assistance. More important, is that you find someone who knows enough about your job, company or industry to provide valuable advice.

The key to finding a mentor is learning how to identify the right person and then *asking for their help.*

CHAPTER 5

Communicating Effectively

Clarify the Message

If you really pay attention, people will tell you exactly what they want. As a corporate writer, I often have to craft a document in someone else's voice. In order to do that, you must learn how to "hear," rather than just listen. Hearing means that you grasp what the individual is trying to say. Asking questions is a good way to clarify that person's message. This same skill will benefit you when your boss asks you to do something. If you are unclear about what is being asked of you, restate what you think you are being told to do. If you are wrong, your boss has the opportunity to clarify his or her request.

A good way to let someone know that you understand him or her is to repeat what he or she said, either verbally or in writing. This lets them know that you clearly "heard" them.

Understand Different Communication Styles

One of the biggest challenges you face when you start a new job or begin working with a different team is that you do not know much about the people involved. An easy way to learn about the individuals you work with is to take the time to listen and learn. Most people have a preferred communication style, and the sooner you figure out how they like to interact with others, the quicker you will fit in. I always recommend that individuals take the DISC Communications Style Questionnaire or at least read up on the topic of communication styles. Here's a short primer on the subject to help get you started.

Each individual has a natural way of communicating. He or she not only speaks using this style, but also often listens from this frame of reference. Communication problems between coworkers often arise primarily because the individuals have different ways of expressing themselves. It's not what you say that causes problems, but how you say it. Learning more about how you communicate and the styles of others will help you improve your ability to work well with peers, supervisors, and subordinates.

I have taken the questionnaire myself. There are no right or wrong answers, so be honest. Successful teams have members with different strengths, as in baseball, in which each person plays a different position. The same holds true in the workplace – effective teams have all four of the styles represented.

The DISC, along with Myers Briggs and other personality questionnaires, is being used in graduate schools and businesses to help form productive teams. I highly recommend that you become familiar with the information below.

DISC Communication Styles

D • Dominance (also known as the Controller)

The Controller is easy to spot because he/she just wants the facts and nothing but the facts. Because of this, they can often be perceived as bossy and insensitive. The Controller is extremely goal oriented, and his/her major motivation is getting things done. He or she will take a project and run with it. Sometimes this person won't even have a plan before beginning, but instead forges ahead with an attitude of "we'll figure it out as we go."

The Controller paints with a broad brush and has little use for details; so don't give out any more details than are absolutely necessary to get your point across. Here are some tips for communicating with a bottom-line person:

- ✔ Be efficient and businesslike.
- ✔ Get to the point.
- ✔ Set and clarify goals and objectives.
- ✔ Give this person conclusions. Only provide details if asked.
- ✔ Solve problems and address objections.
- ✔ Talk in terms of results, not methods.

I • Influence (also known as the Promoter)

You know the Promoter... this person is the life of the party and lots of fun. Promoters love people and love to talk. Their natural sociability allows them to talk for long periods about almost anything. They have an attractive personality and are enthusiastic, curious, and expressive. Here are some tips for communicating with Promoters:

- ✔ Leave plenty of time for talk and social niceties.
- ✔ Ask them about their family, children, etc., and be prepared to talk about yours.
- ✔ If possible, let them "experience" what you are communicating.
- ✔ Talk in terms of people and stories.
- ✔ Use lots of examples.

S • Steady (also known as the Supporter)

The person with a Supporter communication style typically has a low-key personality and is calm, cool and collected. They tend to be patient, well balanced, and happily reconciled with life. Supporters are the largest percentage of the population, and they are typically competent and steady workers who do not like to be involved in conflict. When there is conflict, they may be called upon to mediate the problem. They are good listeners and usually have many friends. One of his or her major motivations is to avoid offending anyone. Here are some tips for communicating with Supporters:

- ✔ Don't come on too strong.
- ✔ Earn their trust in small steps.

COMMUNICATING EFFECTIVELY

- ✔ Don't ask for big decisions right away.
- ✔ Provide plenty of reassurance.
- ✔ Talk in terms of security.

C • Compliance (also known as the Analyzer)

These are the "facts and figures" people. They love to gather details and organize things. They tend to be deep, thoughtful, analytical, serious, and purposeful. Because their communication style includes a need for details, they sometimes hesitate to make decisions if they feel they don't have enough facts. They love lists, charts, graphs, and figures. Because they pay so much attention to details, they can sometimes seem pessimistic. Often they are frugal or economical. Tips for communicating with Analyzers:

- ✔ Make sure you are well prepared.
- ✔ Have plenty of facts and figures.
- ✔ Be prepared for skepticism.
- ✔ Answer all of their questions.
- ✔ Go relatively slow to give them time to think and analyze.

Social Media Do's and Don'ts

Social media can be a powerful way to connect with people and, done right, it is a great way to build your network right from your computer. Revealing too much on social media has become a big problem and has caused many awkward situations, even loss of employment. My advice is not to post anything on a social media site that you wouldn't want to see on the front page of the newspaper or your company newsletter.

Human resource professionals will tell you that social media has made it easier for a company to monitor their employees' activities. Even if the company is not monitoring your actions, most likely someone else in the office will see your posts and pass on the information. This can influence decisions moving forward, and, in some cases, people have lost their jobs. In this age of security breaches, companies might think twice about a person's ability to keep things confidential if that person is overly revealing on social media.

Social Media Do's

- Do join sites like LinkedIn or Plaxio that are oriented toward professional networking. Develop a biography that includes your current and past employment, relevant work, and education as well as your awards, recognitions, certifications, and professional association memberships.

- Do put effort into building your network. Professional networking sites can be beneficial, but you must put forth effort.

- To get started, search for the names of individuals that you know or groups you are associated with, such as your college alumni association. Most people have an affinity for the school they attended and will be willing to connect with a fellow alumnus.

- Begin to send out invitations to connect. If you are reaching out to someone that you know, use the script provided by the site for an invite.

- Once your invitation to connect is accepted, you will see a list of individuals that you might have things in common with and the option to add these names to your network. Review these names and send requests to connect to those you have an interest in adding to your network. For example, target individuals in industries or companies in which you may hope to find a position.

- If you have never met the individual with whom you are trying to connect, write a special note outlining why you would like to have this person in your network. For example, you might say, "I reviewed your profile, and it appears that you have expertise in an area that is of interest to my organization. Can I add you to my professional network?"

- Many people in business development like to list recommendations from former clients and often send out solicitation requests to people in their network. In my opinion, sending requests out of the blue to a former client can be tricky. Receiving a request like this can make some people feel uncomfortable, especially if your relationship is not current. Do not be offended if someone does not reply.

- Do send out updates when you have "news." Social media is a great way to announce a new job, a promotion or new contact information.

- Do use social media when you are looking for a job. However, make sure that you are not soliciting for new work while still employed by someone else. Only do this if your company has announced layoffs and encourages you to find a new opportunity.

Social Media Don'ts

- Do not say disparaging things about your boss or your company on social media.

- Do not reveal company-related information.

- Do not make comments about your coworkers, clients, contractors, or anyone else related to your work.

- Do not talk about or show pictures of yourself getting drunk, doing drugs, or while scantily clad.

- Do not talk about romantic interests in anyone with whom you work, especially if you are having an affair.

- Do not talk about arrests, violence, or stalking.

- Be careful about making jokes and being funny. The reader might not know when you are kidding about driving over someone in the parking lot and take it seriously.

- Do not reveal information about your finances or compensation including how much money you spend or if you are in financial straits.

- Do not post while at work. It is hard to be seen as hard working to your peers if you are posting to Facebook or Twitter 30 times a day.

- Be careful about revealing medical information. If you talk frequently about these issues, your employer might worry that you might make a future disability claim.

- If you are in the middle of a medical insurance claim, do not post photos physically exerting yourself or brag about working out.

- While out of town on company business, do not put anything on social media related to partying, or having a good time.

REFERENCE

Maximumadvantage.com. 2008 Maximum Advantage. August 20,2011 <http://www.maximumadvantage.com/four-styles-of-communication.html>

CHAPTER 6

Bridging the Generational Divide

Communication problems often arise between people from different generations who have a different view of right and wrong. For example: The Baby Boomer generation grew up in an era where books like *Dress for Success* and *7 Habits of Highly Effective People* were at the top of a future manager's reading list. Many still follow these rules.

In contrast, you have the millennial generation which values individualism and tends to be more informal. I hear many complaints about younger generations not understanding the chain-of-command or corporate etiquette. They will handle situations with vice presidents the same way they talk to their peers; older generations see this as a sign of disrespect.

Recently, we had to make a presentation to our board on the winner of a video contest. The winning team made up a song that included the lyrics "down with" and the company name. I suggested that we change these lyrics because it could be construed as derogatory towards the company. A few of my younger employees said, "But everyone knows it means get down." I thought differently. Half the attendees at the meeting would be over 50, and I didn't want to stand in front of a room full of people trying to explain what "down with" meant. You need to know your audience and gear your message to the recipient.

Currently there are six living generations. Each has its own mind set. What was going on at the time they grew up and entered the workforce has a tremendous influence on how they manage employees. Some people are more open to bridging the generational divide, while others are not. It is important to determine which generation your boss came from and whether he or she is willing to look at things in a different way.

Being able to communicate with all age groups is necessary, whether dealing with supervisors, coworkers, clients, or vendors. For example, for older generations pregnancy was hidden so they may feel uncomfortable if a woman comes to work in a tight dress that shows her big baby bump with the "outie" belly button in full view. They will not think you are trendy; they will think you are inappropriately dressed.

The same holds true for business attire. Older generations think that it means a conservative suit, and some younger generations think it means blue jeans and a nice shirt. It is important to learn as much as you can about what the people who influence your career think is right and what they think is inappropriate.

Following is a summary of the six living generation's and details about what each group values. For more information, see www.marketingteacher.com.

The Six Living Generations

GI Generation (The Greatest Generation)

- Born 1901-1926.
- Fought in World War II and grew up in the Great Depression... all leading to strong models of teamwork to progress.
- Their Depression was the Great One; their war was the Big One; their prosperity was the legendary Happy Days.
- They saved the world and then built a nation.
- They are assertive and energetic doers.
- Excellent team players.
- Community-minded.
- Strongly interested in personal morality and near-absolute standards of right and wrong.
- Strong sense of personal civic duty, which means they vote.
- Marriage is for life; divorce and having children out of wedlock were not accepted.
- Strong loyalty to jobs, groups, schools, etc.
- There was no "retirement," and thought you worked until you died or could no longer work.
- The labor union spawning generation.
- "Use it up, fix it up, and make do, or do without."
- Avoid debt...save and buy with cash.

Mature/Silents (The Forgotten Generation)

- Born between 1927 and 1945.

- Went through their formative years during an era of suffocating conformity, but also during the postwar happiness: Peace! Jobs! Suburbs! Television! Rock 'n roll! Cars! *Playboy* magazine!

- Korean and Vietnam Wars generation.

- The first hopeful drumbeats of civil rights.

- Pre-feminism: women stayed home to raise children. If they worked, it was only certain jobs, such as teacher, nurse, or secretary.

- Men pledged loyalty to the corporation; and once they got a job, they generally kept it for life.

- The richest, most free-spending retirees in history.

- Marriage is for life; divorce and having children out of wedlock were not accepted.

- In grade school, the gravest teacher complaints were about passing notes and chewing gum in class.

- They are avid readers, especially of newspapers.

- "Retirement" meant sitting in a rocking chair and living your final days in peace.

- The Big-Band/Swing music generation.

- Strong sense of trans-generational common values and near-absolute truths.

- Disciplined, self-sacrificing, and cautious.

Baby Boomers

- Born between 1946 and 1964. Two sub-sets: The save-the-world revolutionaries of the 1960s and 1970s and the party-hardy career climbers (Yuppies) of the 1970s and 1980s.

- The "me" generation.

- Rock 'n roll music generation.

- Ushered in the free love and societal non-violent protests, which triggered violence.

- Self-righteous and self-centered.

- Buy it now and use credit mentality.

- Too busy for much neighborly involvement yet strong desires to reset or change the common values for the good of all.

- Even though their mothers were generally housewives, responsible for all child rearing, women of this generation began working outside the home in record numbers. They changed the entire nation, since this was the first generation to have their own children raised in a two-income household, where mom was not omnipresent.

- The first divorce generation, where divorce was beginning to be accepted as a tolerable reality.

- Began accepting alternative lifestyles.

- Optimistic, driven, team-oriented.

- Envision technology and innovation as requiring a learning process.

- Tend to be more positive about authority, hierarchal structure, and tradition.

- One of the largest generations in history, with 77 million people.

- Their aging will change America almost incomprehensibly. They are the first generation to use the word "retirement" to mean being able to enjoy life after the children have left home. Instead of sitting in a rocking chair, they go skydiving, exercise, and take up hobbies, which increases their longevity.

Generation X

- Born between 1965 and 1980.

- The "latchkey kids" grew up street-smart but isolated, often with divorced or career-driven parents. The term "latchkey" came from the house keys Generation X kids wore around their necks, because they would go home from school to an empty house.

- Entrepreneurial.

- Very individualistic.

- Government and big business mean little to them.

- Want to save the neighborhood, not the world.

- Feel misunderstood by other generations.

- Cynical of many major institutions that failed their parents, or them, during their formative years and are therefore eager to make marriage work and "be there" for their children.

- Don't "feel" like a generation, but they are.

- Raised in the transition phase of written knowledge to digital knowledge archives. Most remember starting elementary school without computers and having them introduced in middle school or high school.

- Desire a chance to learn, explore, and make a contribution

- Tend to commit to self rather than an organization or specific career. This generation averages seven career changes in a lifetime, not seeing it as normal to work for a company for life, unlike previous generations.

- Society and, thus, individuals are typically seen as disposable.

- Beginning of the obsession of individual rights prevailing over the common good, especially if it is applicable to a minority group.

- Raised by the career- and money-conscious Boomers amid the societal disappointment over government authority and the Vietnam War.

- School problems were about drugs.

- Late to marry (after cohabitation) and quick to divorce...many single parents.

- Into labels and brand names.

- Want what they want and want it now but struggling to buy; many are deeply in credit card debt.

- It has been speculated that they are conversationally shallow because unlike previous generations, they do not have shared media experiences, such as watching movies with family.

- Short on loyalty and wary of commitment; all values are relative...must tolerate all peoples.

- Self-absorbed and suspicious of all organizations.

- Survivors as individuals.

- Cautious, skeptical, unimpressed with authority, self-reliant.

Generation Y/Millennium

- Born between 1981 and 2000.

- Aka "The 9/11 Generation" or "Echo Boomers," America's next great generation brings a sharp departure from Generation X.

- They are nurtured by omnipresent parents, optimistic, and focused.

- Respect authority.

- Falling crime and teen pregnancy rates. However, raised in the era of school shootings, they feel vulnerable even in public spaces formerly thought to be safe.

- They schedule everything.

- They feel enormous academic pressure.

- They feel like a generation and have great expectations for themselves.

- Prefer digital literacy, as they grew up in a digital environment. They have never known a world without computers. They get all their information and most of their socialization from the Internet.

- Prefer to work in teams.

- Have unlimited access to information and tend to be assertive with strong views.

- Envision the world as a 24/7 place; want fast and immediate processing.

- They have been told over and over again that they are special, and they expect the world to treat them that way.

- They do not live to work; they prefer a more relaxed work environment, with a lot of hand holding and accolades.

Generation Z/Boomlets

- Born after 2001.

- In 2006 there were a record number of births in the United States, and 49 percent of those born were Hispanic. This will change the American melting pot in terms of behavior and culture. The number of births in 2006 far outnumbered the number at the start of the baby boom generation, and this generation will easily be larger.

- Since the early 1700s, the most common last name in the United States has been Smith, but today it is Rodriguez.

- There are two age groups: Tweens (8 to 12 years old) and Toddler/Elementary (younger than 8).

- There were an estimated 29 million tweens by 2009.

- $51 billion is spent by tweens every year, with an additional $170 billion spent by their parents and family members directly for them.

- 61 percent of children ages 8 to 17 have a television in their room.

- 35 percent have video games.

- 14 percent have a DVD player.

- 4 million will have their own cell phones. They have never known a world without computers and cell phones.

- Have eco-fatigue. They are tired of hearing about the environment and the many ways we have to save it.

- They are savvy consumers, and they know what they want and how to get it. They are over saturated with brands.

- KGOY ("Kids Growing Older Younger"): With the advent of computers and web-based learning, children leave behind toys at a younger and younger age. For example, in the 1990s the average age of a child in Mattel's (the creator of Barbie) target market was 10 years old. In 2000 it dropped to 3 years old. As children reach the age of 4, old enough to play on the computer, they become less interested in toys and begin to desire electronics such as cell phones and video games.

Words That Drive Supervisors Crazy

Now that you know a little bit more about each of the living generations, let's discuss how certain words can be misconstrued and even push people's hot buttons.

It is amazing how the use of certain words can cause so much trouble, but we all have things that drive us crazy. The sooner you figure out which words your boss dislikes, the better. I had a boss who went ballistic if someone said, "I didn't intend for things to go wrong." He thought it was a cop-out. What he really wanted to hear was, "I should have done a better job ensuring success."

A good example of a word that can be misunderstood is "why." For younger generations, asking "why" is a means of learning how to get things right. For those in the baby boomer or older eras, it sounds as if you are questioning someone's authority. It seems as if the employee is questioning everything he or she is told to do. I suggest avoiding the use of "why" because it makes supervisors feel as if they are being asked to justify themselves.

Here are some alternatives to help you avoid using this word. You could start a conversation by saying, "I want to do a really good job for you, so can I ask you a few questions to make sure I understand what you want?" or "I want to make sure I give you exactly what you need, so can I show you some options?" With these simple alternatives to using "why," the supervisor hears the employee wanting to please, not question his or her decisions.

REFERENCE

Marketingteacher.com. 2000 Marketing Teacher. September 17, 2011 <http://www.marketingteacher.com/lessons-store/lesson-six-living-generations.html>

CHAPTER 7

How to Manage Your Boss

Your relationship with your supervisor is extremely important. He or she controls your happiness in many respects, determining what you work on, how you perform your job, and with whom you interact. In some cases, it is very difficult to "click" with your boss. Tough situations include: not having anything in common, a significant age difference, or being part of a team "acquired" through consolidation or changes in management.

You can choose your friends, but in most cases, you can't choose your boss. Pay close attention to the section below on how to manage your boss for ways that you can improve a less-than-perfect supervisor/employee relationship.

One of the best courses I've ever taken was an Organizational Behavior class in graduate school called "How to Manage Your Boss." Most employees believe that it is their boss' job to get along with them. They are mistaken. It is your job to get along with your supervisor.

A good supervisor is a coach whose job is to develop a team that can accomplish goals. Joining a new work area is like joining a team, and the sooner you learn how things work, the better off you will be. An easier way to look at things is to imagine a puzzle in which each member of the group is a piece. If your shape doesn't fit into the open piece, it is like trying to put a square peg in a round hole. It is an exercise in futility, and all parties will be frustrated. There are plenty of other people willing to bend to fit in. So if you want to keep your job, you need to learn to give the coach what he or she wants.

Building Trust

Once you get to know your supervisor's likes and dislikes, you can start to build their trust in you. For example, as a supervisor, I need to know that my employee is focused on achieving mutually desired results. This is often called "being on the same page." I've learned much of what I know about building trust from my years working in the operations side of the company.

At an electric utility, line crews must work around high-voltage power lines. Before any new recruit can get near a pole, he or she must learn how to work safely and to follow instructions. The two go hand-in-hand. If one person does not follow instructions, he or she could jeopardize the lives of coworkers. There needs to be a high degree of trust before a supervisor will allow an individual to take on greater responsibility.

The same holds true in the office environment. A boss will gradually increase the amount of responsibility given a subordinate based on how well that person handles lower-level tasks. If you can't get a lower-level task done correctly, then why would your boss think you could handle a more important job and not make a mistake?

Recognize Your Supervisor's Style

One of the most common complaints I get from younger people is that they don't "click" with their boss or peers. They feel as if they are not appreciated or well liked. In most cases, the problem lies more in a difference of communication styles than in a conflict between the two individuals. You need to learn how to recognize a person's "style." If you don't, you are speaking different languages.

One of the after-effects of the recession is that companies became leaner and meaner, with supervisors being asked to increase their span of control. This leads to more direct reports and greater responsibility. They are looking for employees who are easy to manage, who understand what they need to do, and who will get things done on time and within budget.

If you require more effort to supervise, there will be problems. As an employee, you are providing a service that your supervisor is paying you for, so you need to give them what they expect.

As both a supervisor and an employee, I have seen what works and what doesn't work when it comes to interacting with your boss. If you keep the following tips in mind, it will be easier for you to develop a productive relationship with any supervisor you work with throughout your career.

Tips for Managing Your Boss:

- **Pay attention to how and when your boss communicates with others.** Does this person like to socialize with employees, either stopping by to get a brief update or chatting while walking down the hall? Or, is the person more formal and prefers that employees make appointments? How often does the supervisor like to meet with employees? Some supervisors might only meet with you once a week, but email back and forth with you a couple of times a day. Other bosses might want to meet with you more frequently. You need to find out what your boss prefers and do things their way.

- **Ask your boss how he or she prefers to communicate.** If your boss prefers emails, then send emails. Don't call on the phone. You need to adapt to the boss' style. If someone prefers short, frequent updates to keep them abreast of activities, and you send a one-page, overly detailed email, he/she is not going to like it. In his/her mind, you are not following instructions, you are giving what you want to give, and this person will not appreciate your effort. In fact, he/she might not even read the entire email. On the other hand, if the person prefers a lot of detail and you give short updates, he/she might think you are not being thorough.

- **Learn to recognize that there are good times to communicate and bad.** We've talked about how to communicate. Now let's discuss when. Timing is everything. If you are reaching out to your boss via phone or in person, ask if it is a good time. If he/she seems rushed or distracted, get right to the point and follow the cues given. If you plow ahead when someone is distracted, then you need to expect it won't be easy. One of my former bosses would tap his hand on the desk as you talked if he was in a hurry. I eventually learned to just turn around and say, "I'll come back later." I knew he wasn't in the mood to talk. Often, receptivity is based primarily on the timing of the request.

- **Learn to find the right opportunity to communicate.** For example, I like to walk around the office and touch base with my employees. The conversation might start with "How was your weekend?" and end with a discussion about a project they are working on. These impromptu discussions are my favorite part of the day, because I get to hear what is going on and get to know my employees a little better. On the other hand, it is not a good time to strike up a conversation when someone is pounding on the computer, deep in thought. As an employee, you need to recognize when it is a good time to talk and when it is not a good time.

- **Give them what they ask for.** This is a biggie. Give your supervisor what he/she asks for and not what you think is needed. To a supervisor, this illustrates an employee's ability to follow directions. The higher you go in management, the more direct you need to be, and you don't have time to elaborate. If your boss takes the time to point out exactly what is needed, then that is what you should do. Meet expectations before attempting to exceed what was requested. In your attempt to "over-deliver," you might come off as insubordinate. Over-delivering is a great quality, but ask your boss questions such as, "Can I do anything else?" or "I have an idea that might add value" before proceeding.

- **Learn how to have a social conversation with your boss.** Many employees make the mistake of talking to their boss only when they have a work-related question. This is like driving a strange car and getting caught in the rain without knowing where the controls are for the windshield wipers. You are always supposed to figure out where the controls for the lights and wipers are before you drive a car. The same goes for communicating. You need to figure out how someone operates before you start doing business with him or her. Start with a social conversation, and see where it goes. One look in someone's office will tell you where his or her interests lie. Does this person have a favorite college sports teams? Is he/she up on current events? Does he/she have a favorite television program or hobby? Does he/she have photos of children and like to talk about their accomplishments? These are all questions you could ask to get to know your boss better.

- **Say "thank you."** Make sure that you don't rebuff your supervisor by not being appreciative. If your boss invites you to a meeting that you normally do not attend, or if he/she gives you an important work assignment, express gratitude for the opportunity. Make sure that your boss knows how much you appreciate the effort to help you. The more appreciation your boss feels, the more willing the person will be to offer you opportunities.

- **Give well-deserved compliments.** Just because someone is the boss doesn't mean that he/she doesn't need to hear when something is well done. This especially holds true after presentations, big projects, or a creative solution to a problem. If your boss did a nice job, say so. Be prepared with a detail, so he/she knows you are sincere. Was he/she thorough, smooth, and compelling? Say so.

- **Ask for your boss's opinion and advice.** Most people like to feel needed and important, and being asked for your advice does both. This is also a sign of respect and is a way to have a conversation in which you can learn about the other person. Asking for advice is an opportunity for someone to impart his or her wisdom and experience. It makes your boss feel like an expert, which will help build a closer teacher/student relationship.

- **Learn your own style.** Certain people are easier to communicate with than others. Usually, it is because you have a similar style or you have developed a relationship in which your styles are complementary. Once you recognize your style and its strengths and weaknesses, you can begin to learn how to broaden your natural tendencies to deal with other types.

Some of my former bosses had strong styles. As a result, I learned to give details to the detailed-oriented person and solutions to the results-oriented person. In addition, there are times to complement someone's style. For example, getting them to pull away from their natural desire for details or to focus on the facts. You do this by knowing enough about yourself and them to find common ground. For example, when I am under stress, I require more facts and data from my staff than normal, because I am focused on results. I will naturally pull in employees who excel in details and decision-making. It is not the time for someone who can't handle a fast pace or lots of facts. On the other hand, when we are developing a creative concept, I like to surround myself with people who can dream and brainstorm. It's not the time for someone to start drilling down to details on each idea. We might go through 20 ideas before getting the three we want to evaluate. Try to determine the purpose of your discussion and act accordingly.

CHAPTER 8

Corporate Etiquette and Professionalism

Whether you know it or not, you are always being watched – in meetings, on the elevator, at business functions, or just walking down the hall – someone is noticing you. Be aware of this, and be sure to put your best foot forward.

The same is true of making a negative impression. Missing deadlines, being viewed as argumentative, overly emotional, negative, calling in sick excessively, showing up late, or even acting disinterested will get you noticed for the wrong reasons.

The goal is for you to be viewed as a professional and capable of sound judgment. Calling too much attention to yourself for the wrong reasons is risky, because you are creating a lasting impression. So, be careful. When your actions say "look at me," others will notice. For example, you want to be known as the person who can gauge any situation and act accordingly, not the woman who has too much to drink at company functions and starts talking very loudly.

Acting in a Professional Manner

How we act at work is extremely important, and different professions have their own circumstances that require certain personality traits. However, most people want to be viewed as competent professionals. Whether you work for a casual, small company or a formal, large organization, you want to be respected and seen as the consummate professional. Below are basic tips that apply to most any industry.

- **Be professional in meetings.** Follow this simple rule to help you gauge how vocal you should be at meetings with superiors: The highest-ranking person in the room should speak the most, so follow that person's cues. Make sure you arrive early and pay attention to the conversation. Sometimes, when you don't take notes, there is a perception that you are not engaged in the meeting, so I encourage you to jot down pertinent information.

  Body language is also important. If you are disinterested, slouched in a chair, playing on your handheld device, or chatting with someone next to you, your superiors will notice.

  Don't bring a laptop to a meeting unless it is required. Do not bring it along so that you can check emails or read the news! It is a privilege to be asked to attend meetings with superiors, and you should treat it as such. If you don't, you will simply not be invited you to future meetings, and your chances for promotion will be limited. Ask the person running the meeting whether it is acceptable to take notes on your laptop. I am one of those people who finds taking notes on a computer annoying. I have found that when you are taking notes on a computer, you are not engaged in the discussion. So, I usually ask guests to minimize typing.

- **Disagreements with superiors should be conducted in private.** Try not to contradict your boss in meetings unless they ask for your opinion. Having someone point out problems or things not done right is never fun, but it is especially bothersome when it comes from a subordinate. You can raise issues, but don't go too far out on a limb trying to convince everyone of your position, especially if it conflicts with the views of your superiors. These conversations are best held in private.

- **Respect the chain of command.** No one likes someone who cuts in line, and the same holds true in business. The supervisory chain of command is there for a reason and should be respected. Each supervisory level comes with a different level of responsibility, and when you go around someone, you lose the value of his or her experience. There is nothing worse as a manager than when your boss knows the status of something and you don't. When you jump the chain of command, your supervisor could retaliate by limiting your interaction with other members of management. So, be careful.

- **Don't drink or use drugs during the workday.** Whether your company does drug and alcohol testing or not, you should never drink or do drugs at any time during the working day – even at lunch. When an employer has a policy about not drinking on the job, that includes lunch, breaks, or even off-hour, work-related situations. It means that you should not be under the influence of drugs or alcohol during any part of the time you are being paid by your employer. If you think that no one will find out, you are mistaken. Your peers notice, and word will get around.

Business Correspondence

With the proliferation of email, it is easier now than ever to send personal thank-you notes, and the like. Email is a timely and efficient way to send messages, but hand-written notes make more of an impression. The bottom line, however, is that something is better than nothing. If someone does you a favor, drop him or her a quick "thank-you." Or if you read about a promotion he/she received or a special announcement like an engagement, send a note of congratulations. Condolences are probably best handled by a card or a hand-written note. Whatever you do, the note needs to be sincere and not form-like. The level of formality depends on how well you know the person and whether you are sending an email or hand written note. Written communication needs to be in proper format and have a hand-written signature. Never send out a hard copy of a note without your signature. Also, keep in mind that over-communicating is just as bad as under-communicating because it diminishes the impact of the note and makes it feel routine instead of special.

To make writing these notes easier, I have provided some samples for your reference. These samples can be used in emails or hand-written notes. If you are sending the note via email, you should always left justify the text.

Sample Hand-Written or Typed "Thank You" Note

Date

Dear Susan,

Thank you for lunch. I enjoyed the opportunity to get to learn more about you and your company and hope we will have the chance to work together in the future.

(Sincerely/Regards/Cordially)

(Your Signature)

Sample Hand-Written or Typed "Congratulations" Note

Date

Dear Susan,

Congratulations on your promotion. I was thrilled to learn that you had been selected as the new director of marketing at ABC Company.

I am sure you will do an outstanding job in the position, and I wish you all the best in your new endeavor.

(Sincerely/Regards/Cordially)

(Signature)

Sample Hand-Written or Typed "Condolences" Note

Date

Dear Susan,

I am sorry to hear about the loss of your father. From what I heard, he was a remarkable man and had a lasting impact on the lives of those around him. Please know that I am keeping you and your family in my thoughts and prayers as you go through this trying time.

(Sincerely/Regards/Cordially)

(Signature)

Professional Attire and Grooming

No one wants to deal with *dress-code issues.* This is one of the biggest complaint executives have about younger employees. I hear it from almost every executive in various industries. No manager enjoys having dress-code discussions with employees, because they are afraid of being inappropriate. Some companies have moved away from corporate casual, because the policy has caused so many fashion mishaps. One of my bosses gave me some great advice: Dress as if you were in the position above you, so that people can "see" you in the position.

Research your company's dress-code policy. If your organization does not have a published policy, talk to someone in human resources or ask your immediate supervisor for recommendations. In general, people should not remember what you wear. If you want to be noticed for your brain, then don't draw attention to other parts of your body. Whether you think it is right or not, people do notice what you wear. When attending meetings or important corporate events, always ask about the recommended attire. At our company, we have started noting it on invitations because of so many fashion mishaps.

Regardless of the dress code, you should always be *clean and well groomed, with coordinated clothing.* The goal is to look as if you take care of yourself. If you want people to have confidence in you, then put some effort into your packaging.

Personal Attire Do's and Don'ts

- Clothes should always be clean.
- Clothes should not be wrinkled or look as if you slept in them.
- Clothes should not be ripped or tattered.
- Clothes should not be overly worn, discolored, or stained.
- Clothes should not be overly tight or revealing. If you want someone to notice your brain, then don't focus on your cleavage or derriere.
- Dress your age, but try not be too trendy. The goal is to look current without wearing something that

might be mistaken for a costume. Just because Lady Gaga wore it on stage, does not mean that you should wear it to work.

- Tights or leggings with a long shirt or sweater are not professional. So don't wear them.

- Clothes should match or look as if they go together. Don't look as if you dressed with the lights off.

- Avoid tee shirts, especially those with a phrase or picture on the front or back.

- Your shoes should not be a safety hazard. Some companies allow flip-flops or sandals, but looking at someone's feet is not appealing.

- Under no circumstances should you take your shoes off, even under your desk.

- Try to avoid excessive jewelry, such as huge dangle earrings, collar necklaces, and multiple bangle bracelets.

- Make sure that you do not have any noticeable body odors. Shower daily, especially after working out. Keep deodorant in a drawer for long days.

- Keep your hair clean and combed. I have hair with a great deal of body, so I can relate to the challenges of a humid day. Keep a brush in a drawer to help keep your hair under control.

- Take good care of your hands. Keep them clean and make sure you keep the dirt out from under your fingernails. However, never clip, file, or polish your nails in a meeting or at your desk.

- Be careful about the length of your fingernails. Claws may be trendy, but your nails should not look as if they keep you from being productive.

- Make-up should not look like you are going club-bing. However, some make-up, such as mascara and lipstick, looks professional. Not wearing make-up can make you look washed out, especially if you have a light complexion.

Types of Attire

There are many categories within "attire," making it confusing as to what is appropriate to wear or not to wear. I will attempt to clarify each of the different types of dress for your reference.

- **Business Attire or Formal Business Attire** is a general term used to describe appropriate clothes for a white-collar, business environment or activity. In most cases, it means that women should wear a skirt suit, pantsuit, or dress. Sweater sets or blouses with a skirt are acceptable. Thanks to Kate Middle-ton, pantyhose are coming back. Women in previous generations are more commonly seen wearing stockings. Pantyhose make everyone's legs look better and present a finished look. The control top style makes you look slimmer.

- **Business Casual or Corporate Casual** is a step down from business attire but a step up from jeans. The term generally applies to social events or meetings with a more relaxed environment, but designed for business. A sweater set or blouse with a pair of pants fits into this category, along with a blouse or sweater with a skirt. Casual dresses apply as long as they are not overly revealing. Avoid spaghetti straps or strapless dresses. Capris that go to the midcalf or below are appropriate, but should be worn with shoes or sandals, not sneakers.

- **Casual Attire** includes blue jeans. Depending on the activity, this might include shorts. I recommend checking with the host before showing up in shorts.

- **Holiday Casual** does not mean jeans or shorts. Clothes in this category are usually festive and include non-business pantsuits, sweater sets, or blouses with skirts and pants, and dresses. As before, be careful not to wear anything strappy or strapless.

The Power of the Pump

Wearing pumps provide a woman with a little something extra in her step. She carries herself in a different way, and she comes off as more confident. Maybe it is being a few inches taller or the fact that maintaining your balance requires you to have greater control of your body. Whatever the reason, I know that I feel more businesslike when I wear pumps. In addition, pumps make your legs look great and add a few inches to your height, which also makes you look thinner.

If you are wearing a business suit or a dress, consider wearing pumps. Even a small heel can make a difference in the way you carry yourself.

CHAPTER 9

Representing Your Organization

Whether at work or attending a function on behalf of your company, you should be a good representative of your organization. First and foremost, employees are extensions of their employer. When you are asked to represent your company, whether at an event, conference or client meeting, you are expected to uphold the values of the organization and behave in a manner representative of the company. Getting drunk, showing up late, or being rude reflect poorly on your company. If your organization does not believe that you can be trusted to represent their interests, you will be sidelined.

Tips for When You Attend
Business Functions and Meetings

- **Minimize use of alcohol at business functions.** My advice to all women is not to have more than one drink at a company function. A former boss of mine once told me that no matter how drunk the boss gets, he or she will always remember how much you drank. He suggested that I drink tonic water with lime. This kept me alert and in control of my actions. Never allow yourself to be photographed holding a glass of any type. Most savvy corporate execs know to either put down their drink or hold it behind their back for photos. Also, remember to hide your purse and take your name tag or badge off during group photos.

- **Bringing a guest to functions.** Whether or not to bring a guest with you to company-related functions poses a dilemma for many women. It could be that they don't have a significant other or their guest might be forced to interact with people that he or she does not know. On weeknights, you may find many executives going by themselves to functions so they can network and do business. It is better to go by yourself and put your best foot forward than to drag a guest along and have to entertain that person all evening. In the second case, neither of you benefits. Weekend events are different. Many people bring a guest, but it is not uncommon for business people to go solo.

Due to children's activities, I am seeing more parents attending both weekday and weekend events by themselves to allow the other parent to cater to their children's after-school or weekend involvements. New trends include bringing older children who might be looking for a job, a friend, a sibling, or a parent.

If you do decide to bring a guest, the same rules apply to their behavior and attire as to yours. They, too, become extensions of your company and should not get drunk or become disorderly. What they do for a living should not be a concern as much as how comfortable they feel socializing.

- **Wait until everyone is served before eating.** It is customary for all guests seated at a table to wait until the last person is served before they begin to eat. This has become increasingly hard, however, with more people making special food requests that cause long delays before the last dish is placed on the table. In most cases, the person making the special request will tell the rest of the guests to begin eating so that their food does not get cold. If the individual does not do this, you can ask that person if he or she minds if the others start to eat, and if he/she says they don't mind, you are free to begin your meal. An additional dilemma is that they serve women first, and there is often a lapse of time before the men are served. A good hotel or restaurant will minimize this time, but in some cases it can be long. Once again, you may ask the other guests whether they mind if the rest of the attendees begin their meal.

Traveling on Company Business

Conferences are designed to be educational, but for many it is an opportunity to have unsupervised fun. Be careful, and follow your instincts. If you think someone is hitting on you, he/she most likely is. I learned this lesson the hard way at an out-of-town meeting. One night, at an event dinner, the married gentleman sitting next to me started making what I thought was overly flirtatious comments. I asked a male co-worker his opinion, and he thought the man was just being nice. The man was "really nice" the rest of the night. I wasn't feeling well, so I sneaked out early and went to my room. The next day, the man came up to me and asked where my room was, because he had looked for me the previous evening and couldn't find me. That was the last time that I didn't trust my instincts.

Two other topics of interest include what to bring on a business trip and how to be safe. Here is more information on both topics:

- **How to pack a suitcase for a business trip.** What to bring on a business trip is just as important as how you behave. Just because you are not in the office or might be in an exotic location does not mean that the rules for corporate attire should be thrown out the window. You are still representing your organization, and you need to look professional. If attending a business meeting, you should dress the same way you would at the office. If you are going to a conference, the first thing you should do is check the brochure for the conference dress code. If you are traveling with a superior, then keep his or her style in mind. If he/she prefers formal business attire, than you should, too. The objective is to fit in and not call attention to yourself. It is better to be a bit over-dressed than too casual. Be careful when meetings take place in tropical locations. Don't be tempted to wear sundresses. Remember that you do business with these people. Don't wear anything you wouldn't want them to remember, such as a bikini, skimpy sundress, or hip hugger pants that show your thong when you bend over.

I suggest that you carry your luggage on the plane so that it doesn't get lost. Buy yourself a nice, dark bag on wheels that easily fits in the overhead compartment. Avoid bringing too many pairs of shoes, because they will weigh you down. Color coordinate your attire so that you can mix and match. If you are traveling to a different country, consult the State Department's web site for the customs of the area you are visiting. Some places have strict rules on what is appropriate for women, such as the Middle East and some Asian countries. You will never go wrong with a conservative suit paired with a set of heels. Skirts should come to just above the knee. Once again, many foreign countries have strict codes, so be respectful.

Always pack some kind of jacket, because meeting rooms are notoriously cold. Check the weather before you leave to make sure you have the appropriate clothing, especially when traveling to areas where there might be snow.

- **Safety tips while traveling on business.** Your personal safety should be a top priority and is made easier by proper preparation, being aware of your surroundings, and staying alert. Through the years, I have compiled my own tips for staying safe while traveling on business. They have worked well for me and are listed below:

- **Spend some time researching your destination.** Using the Internet, your GPS, smartphone or the hotel's concierge, learn the lay of the land. See where your hotel is in relation to the airport and your meetings. The more you know about an area, the easier it is to navigate without getting lost. If you get lost, you could end up in a part of town or on streets that might be dangerous, so take steps to learn the area. Hotels often provide a map of the vicinity at the front desk. Pick one up and get your bearings.

- **Determine your transportation needs in advance.** Once you have researched your destination, you should determine whether you will walk to your meetings, take cabs, or use mass transit. I usually map the routes from each of my locations. This helps when walking from one place to another. In a cab it allows you to provide details to the driver that make it harder for them to take you the long way to your destination. If you plan to use mass transit, allocate a little extra time so that you don't feel rushed. When you rush, you get distracted and may not pay attention to the actions of others.

- **Stay at the conference/meeting hotel.** Staying at the conference hotel makes it easier to get around, and it also offers opportunities to network with other attendees.

- **Ask the concierge for assistance.** The hotel concierge or front desk clerk can be of assistance when you are trying to navigate a city. Don't be afraid to ask them questions, because helping guests is their job.

- **Do not stay in a room near a stairwell in a hotel or near the road in a motel.** Both of these locations are a bit off the beaten path and offer criminals easy access in and out of your room. Do not feel guilty about asking to have your room changed. Your safety is important, and most hotel staff will understand if you tell them your reason for the change.

- **Do not tell strangers your room number.** No matter how nice the gentleman or lady is whom you just met, do not tell that person your room number. He or she can look at the conference schedule and determine when you will be out of your room or pass the information onto someone else. I have heard of cases in which drunken men have shown up at a woman's room for an uninvited nightcap. It makes for an extremely awkward situation.

- **Always lock your door with the deadbolt.** When your door is deadbolted, even someone with a key can't get in. This is an extra layer of security.

- **Bring your cell phone with you to the bathroom.** This might sound ridiculous, but if you slip and fall in the shower, someone might not find you until housekeeping comes to clean the room. I know someone who got locked in the bathroom because of a faulty door. She was trapped for hours until a friend came to look for her.

- **Keep some cash accessible in an outside pocket or change purse.** There is nothing more tempting to a robber than to see a woman pull out her wallet looking for money or a credit card. I suggest carrying a small change purse or putting enough money in a side zipper area of your purse to cover your immediate needs, such as cab fare or tips.

- **Do not take the stairs by yourself.** Empty stairwells, whether in a hotel, office building, or parking garage, can be dangerous. Don't enter one by yourself.

- **Don't let strangers walk you to your room.** Good intentions can go bad quickly when it comes to alcohol and hotel rooms. You might think that someone is being considerate when he or she offers to walk you to your room. It is safer if that person leaves you in the lobby. At a minimum, it looks bad if you happen to run into someone you know, and at worst, it could lead to an uncomfortable situation when you get to the door. You don't want to be accused of leading someone on or being naive.

- **There is safety in numbers.** Just as when you were a child, the buddy system still applies. The more people in your group, the harder it is for a criminal to take advantage of you.

- **Trust your instincts.** If a situation or person makes you feel uncomfortable, it is for a reason. It is better to be safe than sorry. If you find yourself with a group that has different intentions than you do, such as drinking heavily, make it an early evening and go back to your room. If you are somewhere outside your hotel, take a cab. If you do not see cabs in front of the establishment, ask someone at the restaurant or bar to call one for you. Do not walk by yourself, even if it is two blocks.

- **Always have a plan.** Before and during your travel, have a plan. If there is free time, decide what you want to do during this period. If you want to see the sites, research places of interest in advance or ask the concierge for ideas. Always inquire about the safety of such an activity or location of your destination. Hotels don't want to have harm come to their guests, so they will be pretty honest about safety precautions. Try not to "wander" around. It is okay to stroll the streets but have a general idea of the area where you are walking.

- **Stay alert.** When you are alert, it is harder for someone to take advantage of you. Texting or talking on the phone are easy ways to get distracted and disoriented. By the time you look up, you could have walked in front of a car or taken the wrong turn and gotten lost.

- **Don't drink excessively.** Drinking reduces your ability to respond appropriately and makes you less alert. It is easy to take advantage of someone who has had too much to drink.

Proper Place Setting

One of the biggest challenges facing many professionals when they first start to attend corporate luncheons and dinners is familiarity with formal place settings. When the first person picks up the wrong water

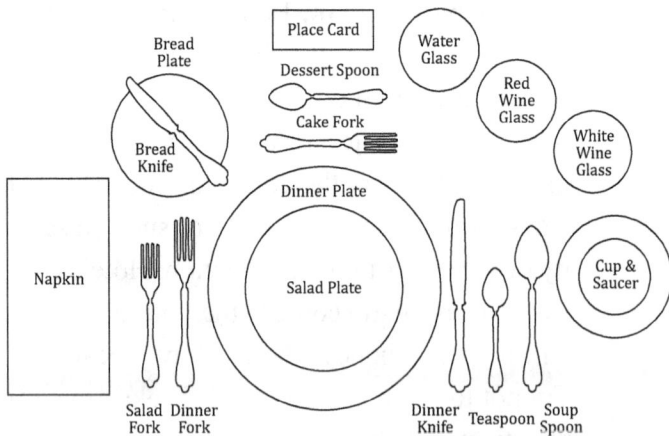

glass or napkin, the whole table is messed up, and it can become embarrassing for the offender.

To make maneuvering through meals a bit easier, I have provided the most elaborate place setting you will encounter. Most meals will include only a subset of the dishes, utensils, and extras shown here. An easy way to remember which utensils to use is that you "eat in," meaning that the outside forks and spoons get used first, and you work your way in. The trick for your butter dish and glasses is to put your two index fingers together with the tips of your thumbs and pull them up to your eyes like glasses. Your left hand resembles a "b" for butter dish, and your right hand looks like a "d" for drink.

CHAPTER 10

Moving Up the Ranks

To move up through the ranks, you need to have all the right ingredients necessary to take on additional responsibility. Your new job needs to be a good fit. Others need to be able to visualize you in the position, or you will not be given an opportunity to progress. One of my former bosses once told me that you need to dress for the position above you, so if a suit is required, wear one. The same holds true for job skills. If the position you want requires excellent planning and organizing skills, you should have strengths in these areas. Often, I will see an individual "pretend" to be someone he/she is not in order to get a promotion. You are not doing yourself or anyone else a favor by doing this. The most successful people are those whose skills align with their job responsibilities.

The Waiting Game

In some cases, promotions are based on a supervisory position opening up or being created, so you have no control over timing. In these situations, it can feel as if you are waiting for water to boil. You are so anxious to get going, and the longer you sit around waiting, the more frustrating it can be.

You are not alone in your frustration, because promotions rarely come on your schedule. They are usually a bit too early or too late. Having been through the waiting game myself, my advice is to stop watching the kettle and find other productive activities to keep you busy. Taking classes and volunteering are two ways to keep from obsessing about your career. They also provide opportunities for expanding your knowledge and gaining experience.

In my case, the longer-than-expected wait was a good thing because it allowed me extra time to prove myself to my peers. I also learned additional skills that proved beneficial when I was looking to move in to management. Instead of just looking at my next promotion, I looked at where I wanted to be eventually – the executive table.

Tips for Moving Up the Ranks

- **Eliminate hurdles to advancement.** Eliminating hurdles that might hinder your ability to obtain a promotion is extremely important and often overlooked. We focus so much on what we want and less on what our company needs. Look at the position you ultimately want. Research the requirements for that position, and look at the work experience of those who have made it to where you want to go. Look at their résumés or, if possible, talk to them. Be informed. I often have young women say to me that they would eventually like to have my job. When I ask them how they would feel about writing 25 percent of the day crafting documents such as annual reports, they look confused. They have never thought about any of the real requirements of my job. Don't fall into the title trap. Find out what a job really requires and what it takes to get ahead at your company.

I knew that I eventually wanted to be a vice president with a seat at the executive table, helping make company-wide decisions. In my situation, most members of senior management had operations or technical experience, a master's degree, and a significant amount of work experience. With this information at hand, I set out to eliminate hurdles by broadening my skills, completing an advanced degree, and undertaking extensive volunteer work to fill in leadership gaps.

- **Broaden your skills.**

  Look for opportunities to learn and grow. One thing that successful people have in common is that they look for opportunities to learn and grow by taking on challenging projects or dealing with problems that need to be fixed. There is tremendous room to prove yourself to others.

  Challenge yourself. Often we are so concerned about doing things right that we play it safe. You need to take risks and try new things. If you are not good at planning, then take on a small project in which you can learn how to be more organized. Do not be happy with the status quo – push yourself.

  Step on every rung of the ladder. When you skip steps, you often lose out on learning the key management skills required at that level. Sometimes we are victims of our own success. Someone demonstrates that he or she is capable, so others start asking to take on higher-level tasks before he/she has mastered basic responsibilities. Your goal should be to fully meet all the requirements of every job you undertake. The more you experience moving up through the ranks, the better judgment you will have when you reach the top. The stakes increase the higher you go, and the room for mistakes gets smaller. Your ultimate goal is to learn as much as you can at each step of the ladder. Skipping steps can be done but only if you are careful.

Being a creative person in an operations-oriented company was not the easiest way to be considered for management. I needed to broaden my experience, and I was looking for a position that would utilize my strongest skill – writing. This would allow me to contribute something to the team, while also learning new things. As a result, I responded to an internal job posting for a training coordinator position in the Electric Operations area. This area was the company's most profitable department and was led by a bright, driven, and demanding vice president. He was highly respected and had a strong record of his employees being promoted to senior management positions.

I knew the job offered an opportunity not only to gain valuable operations experience but to work with all types of people. However, I was concerned that the transfer would take me away from the creative field I loved. I was nervous about the move but knew that I needed to broaden my skills. I ultimately pursued the position.

The next six years were very tough, but gave me a strong foundation on which to build my career. Gaining operations experience was probably one of the smartest things I've ever done because it allowed me to learn a different side of the business and understand our core products: electricity and water. In the operations world, it is all about achieving results. You are forced to become more detail-oriented.

My job as training coordinator involved teaching linemen, engineers, and power plant workers supervisory skills. I would go to the plant and teach power plant workers who were coming off 10-hour shifts. Most were so tired they could barely stay awake. I had to sharpen my presentation skills to hold their attention. Seeing how hard these men worked made me more sensitive to the challenges of craft labor and their needs.

Learning how to work with a wide variety of people is extremely important. Working in a male-dominated environment taught me how to be more direct and to the point and not to take things personally. These are all important lessons after you move in to an executive position.

- **Get an advanced degree.** As a writer, I knew that gaining operations experience would be a benefit, but it wasn't enough to get to the executive table. My boss had gotten his master's in business administration (MBA), and he encouraged many of his employees to do the same. Knowledge of finance and accounting is necessary when you move up the ranks, so an MBA can be beneficial. Getting an advanced degree also gives you a chance to be in a classroom with very bright people who challenge you to be the best you can be, and it builds confidence. Working with individuals from other professions also helps you make valuable contacts and broaden your external network.

  The reverse holds true for women in technical and financial professions. You need to take courses that build the other side of your brain, such as those in marketing and leadership.

- **Use volunteer work to fill in the gaps.** Volunteer work can also help you develop new skills that benefit you at work. Chairing committees is a great way to learn how to manage people, and leading the planning efforts for an event teaches you about project management and meeting financial goals. Volunteering can also help you fill a void in your life. For me, it got me through the years when I was working in a position that was not creative. It made it easier for me to stay motivated. I looked at the entire work/family/social situation and felt balanced.

- **Appreciate demanding supervisors.** I have worked for a number of people throughout my career, and the best supervisors were demanding and tough. Supervisors with high expectations will push you to reach your potential, and after they get you to hit a mark, they will raise the bar. They might not be as warm and fuzzy as other bosses, but they are demanding because they care. They are like your parents. They want you to succeed, so don't fear that they are intimidated by your abilities.

  My toughest bosses could make grown men cry. They were demanding, direct, and results-oriented. There was no "A" for effort. On the other hand, they took the time to develop my skills and encouraged me to become knowledgeable in different areas.

  Then there is the boss who is the nicest person in the world and never raises his/her voice. I had a boss who was jovial, friendly, and caring. Yet the people who worked for him never moved up. Everyone knew him and liked him, but he did nothing to help his employees improve their skills. He never challenged his people because he didn't want them to outshine him.

  As an executive, I work hard at challenging my employees and want them to go home at the end of the day knowing more than when they came in that morning. I can be intimidating, but they have learned to rise to the occasion. My philosophy is to encourage people to take risks while providing a safety net below them in case they face set- backs. It is better to have failed than never to have tried. It is your supervisor's responsibility to provide you with the feedback necessary to improve your skills. Supervisors are only as good as the people who work for them, and the more you prove yourself, the more opportunities will come your way.

- **Take your boss's advice.** Taking the advice of your supervisor is not only logical, but the smart thing to do. When someone takes the time to point out an area that needs development, that person is doing you a favor. It's like walking around with food on your face – wouldn't you want someone to point this out? However, you would be surprised how often employees decide not to listen to their boss and go their own way. Having areas that need development pointed out is not always a fun experience, and you might disagree with your boss' point of view. However, when a supervisor points out these areas that need improvement, that person wants to see behavior change. If you don't change, it will end up on your performance appraisal or be considered when it is time for a promotion. Supervisors do not tend to promote someone who doesn't listen to them.

- **Give your all, and you will gain respect.** My teenaged daughter plays basketball. During her first high school season, she began to get very frustrated because no one threw the ball to her even when she was wide open. She complained to me after every game, and I kept telling her that she wasn't trying hard enough. At one game, my daughter's team played a very aggressive opponent. My daughter got frustrated and started inserting herself more than normal. She started pushing back, and while snatching the ball away from the opposing player, the two hit the ground hard. One of my daughter's teammates extended her hand to help her up and said, "Good job." From that moment on, they threw the ball to my daughter. After the game, I told her that you have to earn your right to have someone throw you the ball. Respect is not given. It is earned.

- **Don't rely on the success of someone else.** This topic was added after hearing from a young man who was disappointed because he had tied himself to the career of an executive who was let go from the company. He felt dejected. He had gone from winner to loser in an instant.

  Tying yourself to your boss' career can be dangerous, primarily because you lose your identity and become an extension of someone else. That person's baggage becomes your baggage, and in some cases, others will think that you were given the position without earning it.

  I have seen people move up the ranks because they are close to an executive. I've been in meetings where a promotion is announced, and there is shock... and no applause. I've seen individuals work hard to try and prove themselves worthy of the title, but it takes a long time to get past the perception of being the "golden" child.

Create your own value. Your skills should be useful to anyone who happens to be your supervisor. You should be known as someone who can work with anyone. In addition, be careful not to use your tight relationship with the boss to your benefit. Making it known that you have special pull makes people angry and jealous. It's like bragging that you are your parent's favorite child.

If you find yourself in this position, you will have to prove yourself more than others. Ask anyone who works at his or her family business. That person will tell you that he/she has to work harder to compensate for any perceived special treatment.

- **Take advantage of opportunities.** It has been said that "good fortune is when opportunity meets preparation." That has certainly been true in my life. Take advantage of every opportunity to make a good impression and learn from others.

  A few years ago, I chaired a committee and was assigned a number of employees of various levels from other departments to work on my team. One woman always volunteered to work on assignments between meetings and was instrumental in putting together our final presentation. She was smart, had a great attitude, and took initiative. She seemed to be a quick study, and even though she was not familiar with my area, I thought she would catch on fast. Two years later, one of my key managers decided to relocate to another state which left an open position in my area. I recruited the woman to work for me. At the time we started the project, neither of us knew that there would be an opening in my area a few years down the road. However, the committee provided the woman with an opportunity to demonstrate her skills to a member of management, and it paid off.

- **Bounce back strong.** In the past year, I have seen two men recover from setbacks and decided to add their stories to this section. In both cases, the men were laid off from director-level positions due to the recession. Each man took a job at my company at a level that was much lower than at his former position. Yet each managed to work their way back up the ranks. In both cases, the men had strong skills and focused on getting results. Their abilities got noticed, and their supervisors looked for ways to promote them and take advantage of their skill sets. Both bounced back strong, and within two years had regained lost territory: One of the men was recruited by a vendor of ours for a position much like his former job, and the other guy just got recruited by another company.

- **Do not whine or take the "Woe is me" attitude.** At the opposite end of coming back strong are people who experience a set-back and then use it as an excuse to feel sorry for themselves. They whine about their plight and want management to right the wrong. They think that the louder they whine, the more they will be heard – that someone will eventually act. That's not the case. No one likes a whiner or complainer. This is not the way to move up in the ranks.

CHAPTER 11

Creating Your Personal Brand

The image and reputation you build over the course of your career is what I call your *personal brand*. Just as for entertainers, politicians, or professional athletes, a strong brand can cut through the clutter and differentiate you from others and get people to consider your product or service. Look at Lady Gaga. Her wardrobe and elaborate performances make her stick out in a very competitive field of female singers, and they have been the key to her success.

Alignment Between the Truth and Perception

The success of a brand requires alignment between what customers value and the truth. The same goes for individuals. Your brand needs to be based on reality, not spin. If there is no alignment, then when the truth is uncovered, the consequences can be disastrous. This has been the downfall of numerous politicians who have built careers based on moral character and then gotten caught doing something that contradicts their image. Consumers can be unforgiving when they are disappointed. They believe that they have been conned. The same holds true in business. There needs to be alignment between reality and perception, so make sure that your image is based on true qualities.

Three Phases in Building a Brand

In 1997, as the head of marketing, I had the opportunity to lead the company's effort to establish a corporate brand, OUC–The *Reliable* One. All my research and experience led me to develop *the three key phases utilized to build a strong brand*: (1) know you, (2) trust you, and (3) choose you.

- **Know you.** Your goal should be to find ways for people at all levels within your organization to learn your name and something about you. You can't choose someone to be on your team if you don't know they exist. So, take the time to strike up conversations on the elevator and offer to help others on projects.

- **Trust you.** When a wide variety of people knows who you are, they will begin to form an opinion of your qualifications. You will need to demonstrate your skills and character. If you consistently do a good job, you will earn trust. When someone begins to trust you, he/she will allow you to take on bigger, more complicated tasks.

- **Choose to work with you.** Once you have earned trust, then you will be in a good position to be chosen for opportunities. However, you still need to make it known that you are willing to help. Don't sit on the sidelines – offer your assistance.

Now that you know the three phases that are necessary to persuade a customer to do business with you, we are going to spend more time on what you can do to create your own personal brand.

As a marketer, I believe that the same elements required to sell products and services are necessary to build a brand for an individual: product, price, promotion, and packaging. I thought it would be an easy way for readers to relate to the topic and begin the process of building their own personal brand.

Steps for Building a Strong Brand

Your **product** is the combination of qualities and characteristics that determine your value.

- **High-quality work and consistency of performance.** The higher the quality, the more the customer values the product. You need to strive for excellence in everything you do. Good enough is not a name brand. It is a "generic." Consistency is also important because you cannot trust someone if you worry that his or her performance level fluctuates. Whether it's a small task or large, you need to focus on getting desired results. Late, incomplete, sloppy work or missing the mark are not acceptable if you want to build a strong brand.

- **Self-motivation is important.** Business has a lot of moving parts, so we tend to prefer to be around individuals who can take care of themselves and are self-motivated. These individuals have high personal expectations and are often harder on themselves than their supervisor. They go about their business without having to be prodded along. On the other hand, you have the "everyone wins a trophy" employees who expect to get an "A" for effort. Their feelings are hurt when their supervisors try to give them constructive criticism, and they get discouraged. It should not be a chore to manage someone. If you have an employee who requires a great deal of maintenance, you will most likely limit your interaction with that person and focus on individuals who are highly motivated.

- **Positive attitude.** When you approach work with conviction and enthusiasm, good results usually follow. Be eager to learn and willing to take on new tasks. Ask, "What can I do for you?" not "What can you do for me?" You need to help others and focus on being a team player. These are important characteristics of winners, and they will help you earn respect from your peers. When you have a negative attitude or are bitter, you are like Linus in the Peanuts cartoon with a cloud hanging over your head. For example, if you enter an elevator and ask someone how he or she is doing and that person begins to complain, chances are that you will not ask the same question the next time you see that person. No one likes to be around Debbie Downer.

- **Focus on meeting, not exceeding expectations.** I know this is contrary to everything you have heard about customer service, but it is true. In most cases, we just want our food cooked the way we requested, and if they add a carrot shaped like a flower, it is nice but does not matter if our hamburger is burned. My favorite example has to do with preparing slides for a presentation. I asked my employees to include a pie chart, because it would best illustrate an important point I wanted to make to the group. They spent hours crafting a beautiful presentation. However, it was missing the pie chart. My first question was, "Where is the pie chart?" My employees said they used something better. In my mind, it wasn't better, so their efforts to exceed expectations resulted in their not meeting my needs.

The **price** is the value of services you provide relative to the market.

- **Give people their money's worth and more.** Product pricing is very important. Consumers have an idea of how much a product is worth to them. It is the same in the workplace. The better the quality, the more someone is willing to pay. I can tell you that whenever we have an employee performance issue, one of the first things I hear a supervisor say is, "For what I am paying them, they should get things right," or "I can find someone who gets it right for less money." Do not price yourself out of the market. I often hear people compare themselves to others or what they think they "should" be paid. I'm sure not many people believe that they are paid appropriately. In many cases, they probably aren't, but it is not a unique situation. I always looked at the different jobs I had as opportunities to gain experience and tried to balance that with pay.

- **Handle salary issues in a professional manner.** If you believe that there is a pay disparity and want to discuss it with your supervisor, I suggest that you handle it in a professional manner. Focus on the job requirements and value of the position instead of how much you are worth. Look for market studies and data to build your case. Beware of giving an ultimatum unless you fully intend to make good on it because you may be forced to keep your word.

- **Look for other ways to be compensated.** Companies are getting creative with compensation and aggregating pay, time off, benefits, and work schedule flexibility to determine the overall package offered to employees. In some cases, they are able to work around existing salary structure limits by guaranteeing a certain amount of overtime to make up for lower pay. Flex time is being used to defray costs for employees with long commutes. This adds up to real savings. Extra vacation time is often something long-tenured employees negotiate when switching companies. The bottom line is to be open-minded.

Promotion and **packaging** focus on projecting a positive image for you and your career.

- **Get noticed for all the right reasons.** You want people to say how sharp and hard working you are.

In many cases, a potential supervisor surveys the workplace looking for good candidates to recruit to their area. On the other hand, supervisors will shy away from hiring someone they believe will require "personal" discussions about appearance, behavior, grammar, and professionalism.

- **Be aware of corporate etiquette and decorum.** Understanding what is appropriate and inappropriate is an indicator of someone's judgment. If you have to watch their every move, then you will be less willing to let them drive the car by themselves. If you have an employee who seems confident, knowledgeable, and professional, you will be more willing to let that person take on leadership responsibility. In business, it is all about getting results as quickly and as profitably as possible.

- **Become known for strong written and verbal communication skills.** The higher you move up the ranks, the more often you will be placed in a position to represent the company, whether to vendors, clients, or peers. You will need to be able to write papers, make presentations, and conduct meetings. If you don't possess good written or verbal communication skills, you should take classes. Toastmasters can help you with presentation skills, and there are numerous online classes offered to improve writing skills. The most important thing is to identify these issues and deal with them early in your career.

- **Master the high-tech/high-touch paradigm.** Appropriate communication is just as important as quality. Knowing what to say, how to say it, and when to say it are extremely important qualities in a manager. With the advent of technology (high-tech), email has become an increasingly important means of communication. Email requires strong, succinct writing skills. No one wants to read a 10-paragraph email or one that sounds like a post on Twitter. At the same time, consumers want targeted, person-to-person attention (high touch). This requires the ability to influence others using a conversation style, not talking at them. Take your time drafting emails, use spell check, and review the message before hitting "send." A tip someone gave me is to not fill in the "to" field until you have completed these tasks. This will help keep you from sending an unprofessional email.

- **Meet deadlines.** Completing work on time is an essential part of a job. If you cannot meet deadlines, it can cause delays further along in the chain. Schedule is often sacrificed to ensure quality. You do not want to become known as someone who is always late finishing his or her work. As a consumer, how do you like it when a plane is late? The same is true in the workplace. You need to be able to get things done on time.

Be thorough and give it your all. There is nothing that gets noticed more than when an employee is thorough. You can tell that person put forth a lot of effort, and you are impressed. This builds confidence in your ability to get things done, and you will most likely be asked to participate in higher-level projects.

CHAPTER 12

Networking and Business Development

Before you can network or attempt to develop business, you need to become proficient at initiating a conversation. There is nothing worse than being stuck sitting next to someone who has nothing interesting to say.

Don't let yourself become boring. Having interests and hobbies provides another dimension to your personality. Travel is a good way to broaden your horizon and expand your knowledge. Learning how to carry on a conversation is also important. It can make for a long meal when you are the one responsible for carrying on a conversation. Asking questions is a wonderful way to engage someone in a discussion. Then, you can sit back and listen, interjecting follow-up questions to keep things going. Below are some easy tips on how to carry on a conversation.

How to Start a Conversation

Are you originally from this area?

How long have you lived here?

What brought you to your company?

What do you do at your company?

Have changes in technology impacted the way
you do business?

Where did you go to school?

Do you have a hobby?

Tips on How to Network

Networking is extremely important and can provide valuable contacts. The more people you know, the easier it is to get things done. I have benefited tremendously from both my internal and external networks. Networking requires taking initiative. You can't meet anyone if you are locked away in your office, so seek opportunities to meet new people.

The peers with whom you work are considered your "internal" network. These will be some of the same people moving up the ranks with you, so get to know them. Having contacts in all parts of the company is smart because you never know when you might need help from another area. Having a strong internal network also opens you up to opportunities to work on projects outside your department. When teams and task forces are being put together, the leader will often be able to recruit members. If you are known outside your work area, you increase your chances of being asked to participate in interesting, cross-departmental projects.

Your "external" network consists of individuals outside your organization. It is always beneficial to know people within your industry and your community, because they can open doors for you in the future. I always recommend joining a good business organization, such as a chamber of commerce or a trade association. Also, volunteering for a committee can provide you with opportunities to meet new people. You need a place where you can interact with individuals from other companies and sharpen your interpersonal communication and networking skills.

Networking teaches you how to build and manage relationships and is a key requirement for all managers who want to lead an organization. The most successful leaders are known for their ability to build strategic partnerships with other organizations and to maintain existing relationships. CEOs must be able to socialize with various groups, including board members, customers, consultants, community leaders, elected officials, and the media. As a leader, you are expected to be a salesperson for your organization. The sooner you start building a network, the faster it will grow.

Tips for building an internal network

- When attending company-related training, get to know as many people as possible. Most participants feel awkward at these activities, and they will be relieved to have someone to talk to during breaks.

- Strike up a conversation while waiting for a meeting to start. Ask the other attendees how things are going in their area.

- Offer to participate in volunteer activities or company committees.

- Support the volunteer activities of your coworkers. There is nothing that endears you more to someone than supporting his or her charitable cause.

Tips for building an external network

- Get to know the consultants and vendors working on projects. Introduce yourself and learn more about what service they are providing the company.

- When attending external meetings or luncheons on behalf of your organization, take the initiative to introduce yourself to others and strike up a conversation. If you have talked for five minutes or more, ask for their business cards. If you see them at another function, walk over and reintroduce yourself.

- Never solicit someone for business while networking at a luncheon. If you do, it might not go over too well. I knew a woman who would walk up to me at functions to say "hi" and then introduce herself to whomever I was talking to. Within minutes, she would be soliciting them for business. She did this with a number of people, and eventually, we began to avoid her at events.

- Walk up to the speaker after his or her presentation, introduce yourself and then ask a meaningful question. Speakers are flattered to have people stick around to ask questions. You can give that person one of your cards and say, "Please contact me if you ever need anything from my organization." Everyone likes to build his or her network – even speakers.

- Building a network takes time, so don't expect to build one overnight. That's why we use the word "building." It is something that you add to over the course of your career.

- Stay in touch with your contacts. Even people you have met 20 years ago can be part of your network. I frequently check in with individuals with whom I went to graduate school through social network sites like LinkedIn and Facebook.

- Using social media is an easy way to increase your network. Recently, a former schoolmate from high school added me to his LinkedIn network. When I accepted, the list of other "you might want to know" names popped up. One of the people listed had experience in an area of interest to my company. I emailed my former schoolmate to get a recommendation and then contacted the individual. As a result, he was added to a bid list for a major project that he would never have known about thanks to social media.

The Benefits of Volunteering

Volunteer work can also open doors for new work opportunities. A friend of mine was recently offered her "dream job" working for a hospital. She had been an active volunteer for years, and when they needed a patient advocate, she was the most qualified.

In my particular case, I became involved in a downtown group that consisted of young professionals like me. The organization allowed me to take on leadership roles, learning how to manage people and meet financial goals. As both chairman of a large-scale event that raised significant money for charity and board president, I had the opportunity to work closely with numerous community leaders and make valuable contacts. All of my efforts were conducted on personal time, but began to benefit my organization. Our company had not previously been active in the community, and having someone so heavily involved in a business group boded well for the company.

Our new CEO was known for his involvement in the community, and he placed a high value on community relations. He knew about my involvement in numerous organizations and established network. My external reputation was strong, and I had just been selected Downtowner of the Year. Timing worked in my favor. He offered me a new position that was being created in the Corporate Communications Department. As a result, I was promoted to administrator of community relations.

Business Development and Entertaining Tips

Pursuing business is much harder than it looks, and so is entertaining clients or potential clients. The goal is to build relationships that could potentially lead to business, so your focus needs to be on the long-term. When you are too eager, it shows and rubs people the wrong way. Being over-zealous is about as subtle as someone hitting on you at a bar using a cheesy line.

Asking a potential client to lunch is one way to begin the process of developing a relationship that might lead to business. Your goal, however, should be to get to know the person. I do not recommend asking them for business at this time. You want the individual to learn about the services you provide and your company, so that if that person or someone he or she knows has a future need, he or she will give you a call. It might take a long time, but if you are highly qualified, the chances are good that this person will eventually refer you to someone or use your services him- or herself. Below are some tips on taking the anxiety out of entertaining while on business.

- **Asking men to lunch.** In some cases, it is tougher for a woman to ask a man to lunch or to be asked to lunch by a male. Some men still feel uncomfortable about having lunch with a woman alone, because they are afraid of the way it looks. Or, they are afraid they won't be able to carry on a conversation for an extended period of time. This is especially the case if you are younger than they are, or they don't know you very well.

  One way around this is to ask to meet for coffee at a Starbucks or similar location. This meeting can be as short or as long as necessary. Another tip is to pick a location that is "busy" and known for business meetings. I never sit in any part of a restaurant that is in any way a "romantic" spot.

  I usually gauge receptivity when running into them in person by saying, "We should go to lunch sometime." If they respond by saying, "Sure, just email me," or provide some level of interest by responding "breakfast or coffee are better for me," then I proceed accordingly. The key is to follow their cues. If they seem to gloss right over this, then don't push it.

If you don't run into them in person, then you can send a short email asking them to meet for "breakfast, coffee or lunch" and let them choose. If they do not respond or say they are busy right now, then don't push it.

- **Picking up the check.** It is customary for the person who issued the original invitation to lunch to pay. However, if the initiator happens to be the client or potential client, the other party could offer to pick up lunch. If you are asking someone for something like a favor or advice, then you should treat. Don't overdo entertaining a client by taking them out too frequently. This could appear inappropriate, and there might be a perception that you have gotten too close to the client. In addition, you don't want to be taken advantage of just because you are a vendor.

- **Abiding by gift and entertainment laws.** Companies, states, and the Internal Revenue Service all have rules concerning accepting gifts and services from vendors and contractors. This is particularly true with elected officials and government employees. Refer to your own company's gift policy when receiving items from vendors or contractors. In most cases, there is a limit to what you can accept, even including food and beverages. If you go over the limit, you might have to declare the gift on your income taxes or on state or federal disclosure forms. This also applies to giving gifts or providing food and beverages to a client or contact. If the recipient does not abide by his or her organization's policies or those of the government, it reflects just as badly on you as it does on that person. Avoid a potentially embarrassing situation by becoming familiar with all ethics policies that might apply.

CHAPTER 13

Business Ethics and Human Resource Issues

Business ethics are more important now that ever. Unfortunately, the pursuit of money has clouded many an executive's judgment and gotten him or her into trouble. The media is full of stories about business leaders who put their self-interest over those of the company. As a result, corporate oversight and regulation have been tightened. In this chapter, we discuss areas that could cause problems for many people.

Purchasing Goods and Services

Most companies have policies outlining how they purchase goods or services. You need to become familiar with these policies and procedures and abide by them at all times. The biggest mistake most people make is by not declaring a conflict of interest. If you have any association with a potential vendor or provider you need to disclose this before the start of the purchasing process. Most companies have policies against being in a decision-making role when it involves relatives, business owners or former employers. There cannot even be a perception of impropriety. Avoid issues by acknowledging your conflict and pulling yourself out of any decision-making situation.

As mentioned in the Networking and Business Development chapter, you should not accept any gifts from a vendor or service provider that exceeds your company's policy. If your company does not have a policy, a good rule-of-thumb is to not accept anything valued over $100. That is the limit set by many state governments and organizations. This includes food and beverage and entertainment-related expenses. An example would be tickets to sporting events or concerts.

Contracts

Most organizations have signature authority levels that apply to contracts and purchases. You need to be aware of what your authority level is before signing any documents or committing your organization to a purchase. Discuss this topic with your supervisor to ensure your compliance. Have a clear understanding of what you can and can't do. Many companies have checks and balances in place that require you to have contracts reviewed by another department that deals with legal issues or purchasing. If your company does not have a policy or process in place, I do not recommend being the only person to review a contract before signing it. An additional set of eyes might catch something that you have overlooked.

Dealing with Awkward Comments and Sexual Advances

Whenever a group of people work together, there is potential for awkward situations. Dealing with inappropriate comments and sexual advances is like walking a tightrope, because if you overreact or underrespond, you could lose your balance and fall.

When I started in business, there were very few females in professional positions. Because women were a novelty, some men did not know how to treat them. Often they flirted or were condescending or both. It was socially acceptable to call a woman "honey or sweetie" or "touch" a woman in an overly friendly way. You were considered "difficult" if you took issue with advances. Things have gotten better, but women continue to deal with these issues ... even when they make it to the top of the organization.

The most important thing to remember is *not to let someone else's actions make you look ridiculous*. These statements and advances are designed to get a reaction from you. The more you make out of them, the happier you make the offender. When you remain calm, you retain control.

In my opinion, there are two categories: Comments and sexual advances.

- **Inappropriate male comments.** When it comes to flirting and making overly nice comments about your appearance, my female friends and I took the approach of minimizing the statements by pretending we didn't hear them or simply saying "thanks." If someone doesn't get a reaction, he will often move on, and an awkward situation is avoided. Alcohol tends to make people feel empowered, so be careful when you are at social functions where there is drinking. Many people will do stupid things and not remember the next day.

I have had to deal with numerous awkward moments with people in influential positions. In most cases, I learned to avoid certain people when they are drinking or huddled with "the guys." This lesson was learned the hard way. I have lived through a few embarrassing incidents.

A perfect example of keeping your cool in a difficult situation with a powerful "admirer" of the opposite sex involves former Secretary of State Condoleezza Rice. During her first trip to Libya, she was informed that Muammar Qaddafi had a "crush" on her and was very public with his adoration. At their first meeting, attended by numerous representatives of both the United States and Libya, the dictator handed Secretary Rice a CD featuring a song he had written for her called "My Black American Rose." She graciously accepted the CD, thanked him and moved on to business. Throughout the entire situation, she remained calm and in control.

If ignoring an individual's comments does not work, then I suggest that you address his actions privately and let him know the comments make you feel uncomfortable and that you want them to stop. If he persists, you should notify your boss.

- **Sexual advances.** Dealing with unwanted sexual advances is probably one of the most difficult things a woman can confront in the workplace. The most important thing to remember is that the behavior of both parties will be scrutinized. You must make it clear that you are not interested or you will be considered a willing participant. Once again, most sexual advances originate during social situations, especially outside the office and where there is alcohol. Perception is reality, so be careful about putting yourself in a position where you are alone with an individual after hours. You must make it clear that you are not interested. If the individual continues to make advances, you should go directly to your boss and Human Resources.

CHAPTER 14

Taking on a Management Role

Now that you have mastered the first rungs of the ladder, you are ready for the big steps: Moving to a management position. As you move up, you benefit more by "coaching" from others than instruction, so I will use more narrative and examples to make my points.

Right Leader at the Right Time

I have always said, "There is a leader for all times." Some people grow companies, and others shore up the foundation. Both types of leaders are necessary at one point or another. The key is finding the right leader at the right time.

You need to ask yourself whether you possess the skills necessary – at this point in time – to effectively manage an area. Are you the "right leader at the right time?" When there is alignment between your skills and what is required, then success will come more easily than if your abilities are not in line with what is needed.

Supporting the CEO

The CEO needs to know you are loyal to him or her and the organization. You should always "respect the position" even when someone is new and might not yet have mastered the company's unique ways. However, be careful about being perceived as too attached to a CEO, because things change. Focusing on getting results and making yourself a valuable member of the team allows you to be an interchangeable part, able to deal with the transition to a new leader with flexibility and openness – two things a new CEO looks for in subordinates.

The Management Pyramid

The higher you go, the greater your degree of control, so you need to master different skills. Imagine a pyramid. When you are a first-line supervisor, you are responsible for physically doing the work. There are many of you. If one person makes a mistake, there are others to pick up the slack. Each layer of management provides protection. As you move up in management, you must widen your vision. You need to look ahead, which requires the ability to plan and motivate others to meet goals and objectives. The higher you go, the fewer layers of protection and the more responsible you are for the actions of the people below you. This is why CEOs have employment agreements. They can be fired for mistakes made by anyone below them.

Once you decide that you want to take on a leadership role, you should prepare yourself for the challenges that come with the position. I have had the opportunity to work for some great leaders and some not-so-good ones. Two qualities that effective CEOs should have are perseverance and the ability to handle risk. A former boss told me, "You can't tell if someone is a good leader until you see how they handle failure." For some people, experiencing failure is a fatal blow, and for others, it is an opportunity to learn and improve.

Moving into management is not easy, and some will find the transition harder than others. One of my favorite quotes about leaders is: "Managers do things right, and leaders do the right thing." The higher you go, the more you move from "managing" to "leading."

Over the years, I have learned a lot of lessons about leadership, both through experience and by listening to others. I hope that these tips will help as you take on an increased management role at your company.

Qualities of a Good Manager

- **Know the difference between doing things right, and doing the right thing.** You have probably heard the saying "No guts, no glory." This is especially true in management. Being a leader means that you have the ability to take risks and fight for what you think is right. Some of the world's greatest leaders, like Winston Churchill and Abraham Lincoln, were willing to risk their careers to lead their countries to a better place. They were not perfect and suffered numerous failures in their lives. However, they learned from these lessons and grew smarter and stronger.

    If you are overly concerned about always doing things right, you will limit your ability to learn and grow. Mistakes allow us to identify bumps in the road that teach us what to avoid in the future. Weighing risk and reward is necessary, but letting caution keep you from moving forward or being creative can limit your ability to motivate others and maximize value for your organization.

- **Interest in learning from others.** One thing I've done throughout my career is learn from the people I work with, report to, and admire. Most people will be flattered when you show interest in hearing their story, and if you listen to them, you will benefit from their experience.

- **Seek guidance from people who have strengths in areas where you want to improve.** I learned many valuable tips from my peers, bosses, and CEOs, including how to manage employees, solve problems, and think strategically. Each of the individuals had strengths in areas where I felt deficient. For example, one of my peers led a large department with numerous employees at various levels. He was known as a great manager of people. Whenever I found myself with an employee issues, I would call him and ask his opinion. He even coached me through dealing with male vendors who were giving me a hard time. His advice not only was beneficial, but also it built my confidence. I knew that he was there to lend support. As it turned out, he was eventually promoted to CEO and became my boss. The rapport that we established earlier made his transition to a boss/subordinate relationship much easier, providing me insight into how he likes to manage people.

- **Benefit from the experiences of those you admire.** Another way to increase your knowledge about successful management is to spend time with people who are good leaders. Putting yourself in a position to hear their stories and showing interest is a good way to benefit from their experience. For example, one of my former bosses was known for being strategic and a master at politics. He was a great storyteller and by the end of a typical week had racked up some interesting experiences and was eager to talk. I will always remember Friday afternoons with Bob. We sat in his office, and he told me about his adventures, always being sure to point out the political lesson in the story. I used to call these anecdotes his "master of the universe" stories. He would tell me about the behind-the-scenes deals he made, ensuring that he did not call attention to himself. He would quote the political saying "The real power belongs to the people not mentioned in the story." Spending this time with my boss taught me a lot, and it also strengthened our working relationship. Look for ways to learn from others.

- **Read about famous leaders in history.** Reading about the experiences of famous leaders in history is a great way not only to learn, but also to expand your horizons. As you move up in management, you will be placed in situations, whether socially or through business, that require you to have meaningful conversations about things other than work. Many highly successful people read non-fiction and focus on books about events or leaders in history. If you want to be able to contribute to these conversations, start expanding your reading list.

- **Stay abreast of current events.** Understanding what is gong on in your industry is necessary to being a successful leader. You are expected to be an expert in your given area and should be familiar with the latest trends and emerging technology. When others know more about your area than you do, it is dangerous. Eventually, they will want to get more involved in setting strategy and priorities for your department.

Staying abreast of politics and current events is also essential, because you will often find yourself at luncheons, dinners, or meetings where what appeared in the news that day will become the topic of conversation. In addition, the more you know about a variety of topics, the easier it will be to strike up a discussion with others. For example, I recently read books about Paul Allen (co-founder of Microsoft) and Steve Jobs (co-founder of Apple) to better understand emerging technology trends. Both books taught me more about information technology that will allow me to anticipate emerging trends that will impact the way we communicate with customers. If you don't like to read, invest in books on CDs or tune into talk radio and listen while commuting.

- **Capacity to deal with high levels of stress.** The higher you go in an organization, the more stressful it will be. You are responsible for the actions of others, achieving results, and meeting deadlines while staying within budget. It becomes increasingly more difficult to leave your work at the office and not take it home with you. Stress can affect your health and happiness, so you need to learn how to manage it. Exercising regularly, eating right, and getting enough sleep are three things you can do to minimize stress. Another tip is to stop looking at your hand-held device at a certain time of the evening. This will allow you time to relax before going to bed.

- **Ability to remain calm under pressure.** The higher you go, the more important it is for you to handle pressure. Often, you will find yourself in a tough situation that requires you to stay calm and guide your group to resolution. Imagine yourself as the pilot of a plane – when you hit turbulence, the passengers on board want to know that the leader will not panic but get them to safety. Some people are at their best when they have their back against the wall. Not only do they find a way to get themselves out of a tough situation, but they turn it around to their benefit. Getting emotional, panicking, having a temper tantrum, and blaming others are not productive ways to deal with problems. If you need to blow off steam, close your door or go for a walk until you are ready to tackle the situation.

- **Know when you need to turn up the temperature.** The other side of staying calm is knowing when you need to turn up the heat. The example I always use relates to disciplining a child. A parent must react differently in dangerous situations, such as when a child chases a ball into the street without looking for oncoming cars than when the child makes a simple mistake, like spilling a glass of milk. The same holds true in management. There are times when you need to turn up the heat to send a signal that the infraction is serious. The frequency with which you have to do so with an individual is an indication that you probably have a problematic employee. Be aware of this.

- **Wherewithall to handle disappointment and loss.** There are many types of changes that you will deal with in your career, both pleasant and challenging. When the good things, such as promotions, come along, handle them with maturity and don't gloat. When you face tough ones, try to find a time when you can get away from everyone and let your feelings out. It's okay to feel sorry for yourself for a while in order to deal with the situation. Go for a walk and cry or vent to a friend or family member

Just don't hold it in, because it will eventually eat you up.

- **Handling Disappointment.** When things don't go the way you anticipated, it can lead to disappointment. Perhaps you didn't get the promotion you wanted, or a key project was assigned to someone else. These are things that can get you down and sap your motivation. If the situation involves another individual, do not get bitter and hold a grudge. That is not a productive use of your time. As they say, "success is the best revenge." Focus on setting new goals and moving forward.

- **Coping with crisis.** Sometimes you suffer a loss, and you must rise to the occasion. Many people have to deal with the loss of loved ones or divorce, but you cannot let it affect your work. It isn't easy, but you have to take it one day at a time. Having lost loved ones and gone through a divorce, I understand how difficult it can be not to let the situation affect your work. Let your supervisor know that you are dealing with a loss or a tough situation and apologize in advance if you seem distracted. This will let them know why there might be changes in your performance. If you are having trouble coping, then seek professional help. There is nothing wrong with getting counseling and many companies have an employee assistance program

(EAP) to provide help in times of need. The goal is to make yourself feel whole again.

Things a Good Leader Should Know How to Do

- **Learn what motivates people.** All employees are different. For example, I once had three employees all motivated by different things. The first person was a very strong writer and needed frequent positive reinforcement. The second employee didn't need compliments but was, instead, motivated by money. The third subordinate liked attending seminars where she could increase her knowledge and develop new skills. As a manager, you should learn what matters to your employees so that you know how to keep them motivated. This will also help you give the right reward to the appropriate person. For example, providing an employee with an office with a window can matter a great deal to one person, while another might prefer an opportunity to earn overtime. The point is that everyone is different, and a good manager takes the time to figure out what makes his or her employees happy. A happy employee is a productive employee.

- **How to make decisions.** There is nothing worse than a supervisor who cannot make a decision. The inability to make up your mind on how to proceed not only slows down work but also frustrates those around you. Management requires the ability to analyze risks and rewards, costs and benefits, and then decide how to move forward. If you can't decide how to take action, you should not be in management. The higher you go, the more frequent and more difficult the decisions.

- **Voice your opinion.** Having an opinion is also important. Ronald Reagan once said, "If you and I agree on everything, then one of us is not necessary." Good leaders surround themselves with smart people and listen to them. A manager will expect subordinates to offer advice and recommend a course of action. Sometimes you do not have a lot of information to go on, and you wish you had more time or facts, but you don't. You are paid to make decisions, and you cannot be afraid of risk. Your opinion might be different from your boss'. If you want to be effective, you need to be able to defend your position, even if it conflicts with that of those around you. For maximum results, pick the right time and place to voice opinions. Private conversations usually offer the best environment for discussions about differing opinions. People appreciate "passion" more than they do being "corrected." Focus on benefits instead of being critical.

- **Get results.** Gain a reputation for getting results. I have seen good supervisors fall into the trap of either "analysis paralysis" or biting off more than they can chew. Taking too long to plan and analyze can earn you a reputation as someone who can't get things done. On the other side is the individual who routinely makes decisions too quickly and backs him- or herself into a corner.

One of my favorite stories concerning results comes from Mayor of New York City Rudolph Giuliani in his book *Leadership*. Giuliani talks about his first few months in office. He knew he needed to let constituents know that he was committed to getting results and turning the city around. He decided to fix a small problem that could be addressed quickly. This would buy him time while he worked on bigger issues like reducing crime and spurring economic development.

New York City had a problem with "squeegee guys," men who would walk up to your car when you were stopped at a light and start to clean your window. They would then seek payment for this service. If you didn't pay them, they might damage your car. People hated stopping at lights because of the uninvited window washers.

The Giuliani administration did some research and found out that many of these people were skipping out on parole. Police officers could not arrest people without cause, and it was not against the law to clean windows. Instead, they came up with a legal way to approach the squeegee guys. They decided to pass an ordinance requiring a permit to operate on the street. This allowed police officers to approach them to check their permit. Within days the squeegees were gone. They knew that if a police officer ran their ID, they would get caught skipping out on parole and risked being arrested.

New Yorkers were jubilant and realized that Giuliani knew how to get results. My advice to you is to find your "squeegee" problem and fix it. Get something done that matters, and you will gain support from your subordinates, superiors, and peers.

- **Surround yourself with good people and listen to them.** A former long-time CEO at my company used to say that the key to his success was that he surrounded himself with good people and listened to them. No one is perfect, so it is imperative that you have subordinates who are highly qualified. Two or more people working together productively form a synergy, and the whole group becomes more effective than the individual members alone. Ideally, these people should have a skill set that compliments yours. For example, if you are not good with details, you should make sure that there is someone on your team who has these skills.

Surrounding yourself with good people is probably easier than the "listening" part. You need people on your team who are not afraid to tell you the truth. We all need someone who will keep us from driving off a cliff. Different points of view are healthy, so pick your employees wisely and then encourage them to voice their opinion.

- **Help others when they need it.** Providing your peers with assistance is a great way to strengthen a relationship and build trust. It also increases the perceived value of your department, which benefits everyone. The higher you go, the more favors you should be doing for your peers, especially when they are running up against a tight deadline. You want to be the person your peers turn to in their time of need.

- **Learn from your mistakes.** I always tell my employees that *mistakes are an opportunity to learn and make improvements*. Sometimes, it takes burning your hand on the stove to realize that it is hot. We can all remember things we have done in the past that did not work out well, and hopefully, we learned what "not" to do the next time. In addition, making mistakes as you are coming up the ranks can teach you valuable lessons when the consequences are smaller. These are thousand-dollar mistakes instead of million-dollar ones.

  We all make mistakes, so the most important thing is not to make the same one twice. As the saying goes, "Once a mistake; twice a habit."

- **Take responsibility for your actions.** Everyone makes mistakes. However, *it is what you do after the mistake that everyone remembers*. Those who are honest and forthright fare much better than those who don't take responsibility for their actions. It is also better if you inform your boss of the mistake right away so that he or she can help fix it, rather than waiting until they find out for themselves. I learned early in my career managing media relations that you need to "make it a one-day story" and "deliver your own bad news." You do this by being honest, admitting your mistake, committing to solving the problem, and opening yourself up to solutions from others. If you do this, you will gain respect from your peers and superiors. Don't blame others and deny responsibility. It is hard to trust someone who does not admit his or her mistakes or walks away from a problem, expecting someone else to fix it.

- **Ask for help.** Imagine yourself stepping into quicksand (making a big mistake). Is it better to ask someone for help or attempt to struggle out by yourself? The same holds true when you have done something wrong. Good leaders know when and how to ask for help. They find the people most qualified to provide assistance, and they listen to them. If you make a mistake, admit it, and be proactive about finding a solution. It will be embarrassing for a short time, but you will recover. Remember: make it a one-day story.

Unfortunately, many people are afraid to ask for assistance because they worry it will make them look incompetent or weak. When you hide problems, you run the risk of letting them get bigger and harder to fix. What they end up doing is digging a deeper hole. As one of my coworkers often says, "When you are in a hole, stop digging."

- **Become comfortable having tough employee discussions.** One of the hardest parts about being a manager is dealing with employee issues. From performance to work habits, it is not easy to initiative these types of conversation. Keep in mind that you are not doing anyone any favors by avoiding tough discussions. Overlooking these issues can lead to bigger problems. Most likely if you have noticed a problem, others have as well. Your inaction will lead to a lack of respect by your subordinates. As they say, "discipline is love." Providing feedback to an individual on his or her job performance gives that person an opportunity to improve. You cannot be an effective leader if you are not comfortable having these discussions. Another word of advice: hold these discussions in person, not via voicemail, email, or text.

- **Be able to move on after a heated discussion.** One of the things I admired about a previous boss was his ability to have heated discussions with people and then go play golf as if nothing happened. Being able to have a confrontation and move on is important. In business, things can get tense, especially when you have a different opinion from someone else. Trying to air your differences and have a meaningful discussion sometimes leads people to lose their tempers. Try not to take this personally.

One thing I have learned to do when there is no meeting of the minds is to "agree to disagree." In this case, no one loses, and it is easier to put the situation behind you.

- **Don't hold a grudge.** One of the hardest things about business is that things don't always go the way you expect. Holding a grudge against a person or a business can lead to missed opportunities or, in some cases, wasting time obsessing about getting even. You need to learn to let these feelings go. In Chris Matthew's book *Hardball*, he describes this as "not letting someone rent space in your brain for free." It means that when you hold a grudge against someone, you let him or her take up valuable time that could be used on more productive matters. Your time is worth money, so don't waste it on things that don't matter.

- **Avoid conflicts of interest.** Most companies have written conflict of interest policies. You should be knowledgeable about your organization's ethics and purchasing guidelines to ensure compliance. Many careers have been ruined by not abiding by rules involving interaction with vendors. A boss of mine once told me that whenever you eat a meal or have a drink with a vendor, whether by yourself or with a group, your name will appear on their expense account. I knew someone who lost a job because a project she was running ran over budget and she went to lunch frequently with the consultant working on the project. There was a perceived lack of supervision because she spent too much time socializing with the vendor. The vendor had taken her to lunch frequently at expensive restaurants and expensed the charges. The company policy clearly stated, "Managers need to avoid perceived conflicts of interest when supervising vendors." As they say, "There is no such thing as a free lunch." Whenever a vendor or consultant picks up lunch, he or she is going to expense the meal. It creates a permanent record, so be careful not to dine with contractors too often.

The other issue that gets many people into trouble is doing business with friends. This is always tough, and some people are better at managing these relationships than others.

Before you consider doing business with a friend, you need to ask yourself if you would be willing to fire that person if you had to. If you can't say with 100 percent certainty that you could, then don't hire that person.

- **Apologize, and say, "Thank you."** I think most of us would agree that "I am sorry" are three of the hardest words to say, especially in business. Learning how and when to say them is important. The higher you go, the more you will be expected to be able to apologize on behalf of your subordinates or the company. Apologizing can stop a negative situation from escalating. When someone apologizes in a meaningful way, it is hard not to calm down. It also helps clear the air and allows you to move on in a productive manner. However, avoid adding "but" after saying you are sorry. It does not sound sincere, and it comes off as an excuse.

You should only say you are sorry when you truly mean it or when it is necessary. My former boss was a master at apologizing and often used humor to break the tension. He was a big guy who used a cane because of multiple back surgeries. Once he made a city council member very angry because he supported her opponent in an election. She was an older woman, and they had known each other for a very long time. After she won re-election, he walked into her office and said he was there to "beg for her forgiveness." She yelled for a while and then forgave him – relationship saved.

Executives should not only be able to apologize but also to say "thank you." This is especially true when dealing with employees, customers, or clients. A customer who spends money with your organization wants to feel appreciated. Saying the words "thank you" is an extremely important way to show you recognize that the individual and/or organization has done something to your benefit.

You should be able to show gratitude in a meaningful way and not because it is required. It needs to be sincere, and the more detail the better. For example:

Thank you, ABC Company for sticking with our organization even through tough times. We appreciate your business and will do whatever it takes to continue to provide you with the highest level of service.

REFERENCES

Chris Matthews. <u>Hardball.</u> New York: Simon & Schuster, 1999.

Rudolph W. Giuliani. <u>Leadership</u>. New York: Hyperion, 2002.

CHAPTER 15

The Value of Experience

One of the best seminars I ever attended was on crisis communication in New York City after 9/11. The keynote speaker was from American Airlines. I asked her how the company dealt with having planes being flown into the Trade Center, killing thousands of people. The speaker said that the senior management team consisted of long-tenured, highly experienced employees who had dealt with other plane crashes. As difficult as the situation was, these executives had gone through numerous smaller crises that had prepared them for dealing with a tragedy of this scale. To me, this exemplifies the value of experience. It is important to learn how to deal with problems throughout your career because as you move up the ranks, the issues will get bigger.

Practice Makes Perfect

In 2004, Orlando experienced three major hurricanes within 45 days of each other. The first one, Charlie, changed course at the last minute and hit our town. Within half an hour, 85 percent of our customers lost power. When the storm finally passed at 9 p.m., we were afraid to walk outside because we didn't know what to expect. I remember the look of disbelief on our faces as we saw 100-year-old trees tangled in utility lines lying across streets and on top of houses. Cell phones were down, along with other forms of communication, including television. You can't run a television or computers without power, and many customers had landline telephones that required electricity to function.

My staff and I were responsible for communicating with customers using only the daily newspaper and minimal radio. We pulled together a team of a hundred non-essential employees from our company and the City of Orlando to walk neighborhoods and distribute flyers. Board members walked door to door to let customers know the status of power restoration. It was like the dark ages, and we were forced to adapt.

A week after we restored power to everyone, Hurricane Frances moved through Orlando, and we went through the entire process again. We learned a lot of lessons after the first storm and improved many of our procedures. By the time things settled down after the second hurricane, a third one was moving our way. I remember getting the phone call alerting me to the storm's path toward Orlando. I was flabbergasted. However, by the time Hurricane Jeanne hit, we had perfected our processes and procedures. After dealing with the three storms, we had done a year's worth of work in 45 days and garnered more on-the-job-training than we could have ever imagined. And the post mortum evaluations allowed us to codify lessons learned.

We have not had storms that large since 2004, but the lessons learned have helped us deal with other types of crises. After you do something the first time, the second time should be easier. The same holds true in business.

This is especially the case when dealing with employee issues – *practice makes perfect*. You need to learn how to work through awkward situations at a lower level before you are faced with a big issue, such as dealing with a potential workplace violence issue or with someone who becomes disruptive. Learn along the way, not when you get there!

CHAPTER 16

Having Children While Working

Having children is a life-changing experience and one of the single most challenging things that any woman can do. I have been blessed with two daughters and they have enriched my life. It hasn't been easy working while being pregnant and raising children, and the decision to do so should not be taken lightly. However, it is possible to excel at being a mother and a manager. In fact, I have found that motherhood and management require many of the same skills.

As I mentioned at the beginning of the book, assessing yourself and what you want your future to look like includes whether you want to have children. I had planned to quit my full-time job and be a consultant when I had my kids, but things did not work out that way. At first, I kept working because my employer offered health insurance and my husband's did not. I got divorced when my children were only one and three, which was also unexpected. Needless to say, the next decade was filled with trying to keep many balls in the air.

My children are now teenagers, and the oldest is looking at colleges. They are great kids, and we joke about all the times I was late picking them up or forgot to make cookies for snack day, although they do remind me of these incidents when they want something.

In this section, I will try to pass on some of the things I learned while having children and working. Most important, you should know that you are not alone. Other women feel the same way you do and struggle with balancing their desire to be a good mother while continuing to move forward in their career.

Timing Is Everything

One of the questions asked most frequently is how long someone should wait to get pregnant after beginning a new job. My response is that it is not fair to an employer or the people around you if you get pregnant within the first year. In the first year, an employee is still in the process of proving herself and will not have built up enough equity to start taking from the goodwill bank. The more valuable you are, the more willing your employer will be to work with you on flex time.

Having a child while working requires the ability to put the needs of someone else above yours, even when you are having a bad day. Murphy's Law is always at work, and your child will probably be up sick the whole night before you have a huge presentation. In fact, sleep becomes a luxury, along with the new purse you have been eyeing for months. Keep this in mind when deciding to have children. The more you are mentally ready for the change, the better. Make sure your partner is prepared, too. Ideally, both partners should be willing to carry the burden of caring for children.

Managing Stereotypes and Perceptions

The workplace has become more accepting of pregnancy than when I had my children. In fact, many men are taking paternity leave, which has leveled the playing field a bit. But employers still worry that a woman will quit her job to stay home with children or not be able to pull her own weight. Some older supervisors might even think you should quit your job and stay home with your kids. Overcoming these perceptions will require you to maintain a professional demeanor and not ask for special consideration. Women can be less sensitive than men when it comes to accommodating pregnancies. I remember hearing women who had no children complaining about having to cover for those who did while they were on maternity leave. In fact, hearing how you were up all night because the baby couldn't sleep does not garner much sympathy. If mentioned too often, especially when you are facing challenges at work, it can be seen as an excuse for poor performance. Some may be thinking to themselves, "You made your choice, deal with it" or "I did it, so can you."

Every woman I have worked with, managed, or interacted with at my company who has had children while working has done an outstanding job of excelling at her position while balancing her personal life. They did not skip a beat. They never used their pregnancy as an excuse and fulfilled the obligations of their job while out on leave and when they came back. As a result, pregnancy is not seen as an issue.

However, one bad experience can ruin it for others, though. Many years ago, I hosted an association board meeting at my building. One of the attendees came in with her baby in a stroller. After the meeting ended, I was confronted by a number of women at my company who thought it drummed up negative thoughts about mothers in the workplace. They were right. Later that day, I heard a man ask whether our female employees were going to start bringing their children to work. All it takes is one person doing something that reinforces a perception or stereotype, and it makes it hard for the others.

The Generational Divide

We have talked in an earlier chapter about the Generational Divide, and it plays a big role in how people view pregnancy and having children while working. Some bosses and peers will be predisposed to what the "norm" was when they came up the ranks. Keep this in mind, and don't take any comments personally. For example, I had my first child in 1994, when many professional women hid their pregnancies for as long as possible in fear of being sidelined or not taken seriously. We did not talk about doctor's appointments, sonograms, Lamaze, or anything else related to having a child. In fact, we wore baggy clothes to hide our "bump." If you have a boss who does not seem to share your enthusiasm for your pregnancy, it might be because it is not what they believe is the normal way to handle the situation. Be careful not to make them feel uncomfortable.

Women who had children in the 1980s and 1990s might not have been given the opportunity to telecommute or use flex time and might feel some resentment that you have it easier. This is especially true if they had already moved to a management position. By the time my second daughter was born, my career had taken off, and I was a director. It is no secret that the higher you go, the harder it is for anyone, female or male, to take an extended period of time off. Many of us working at this time were still relying on landline phones and fax machines for communication. This made it harder to stay connected to the office, so employers were anxious to get you back to work. In both of my pregnancies, I was brought work to approve while still in the hospital after the birth of my daughters. Many other women in my generation faced the same challenges. If they are not overly sympathetic, it probably has to do with the fact that they think you should be able to tough it out just as they had to. This scenario is similar to hearing your grandparents say, "I had to walk two miles to school in the snow, so you should, too." It is not a matter of not being sensitive, as much as holding you to the same standard they had to live up to.

Dealing with Working Mother's Guilt

Many working mothers feel guilty about not staying home with their children. They worry that their child will be negatively impacted by not having a mother around all day. In some cases, they may feel selfish for not wanting to sacrifice their careers to raise their kids. For those of you feeling the guilt, know that you are not alone. Many other working mothers feel the same way you do and struggle with their emotions every time they have to drop their child off at day care. Or worse, some women don't feel guilt taking their child to day care, but feel guilty because it doesn't bother them. Whichever applies to you, rest assured that there are many others out there struggling with the same feelings. You worry that your choices will negatively impact your child. As a single, working mother, I always worried about my children becoming a statistic and hearing others say, "What did you expect?" However, as a mother of two well-adjusted teenage girls, I can assure you that your children can thrive under the care of a working mother.

The most important thing to remember is to have reasonable expectations. I know it sounds cliché, but children do prefer quality time to quantity.

Here are some tips picked up through the years of working while raising my children:

- **Establish routines and schedules.** A child feels secure when he or she knows what to expect. This also makes it easier for you to manage priorities and get things done. Establishing routines makes it easier for children to transition to a time when they have to be more independent. If they spent their early years knowing that they always came home from school, did their homework, ate dinner, bathed, and then read a book, they may begin to see this as normal behavior and stick to the schedule without your prodding.

- **Eat dinner together.** It doesn't matter what you make for dinner as long as the family sits down together. You can tell a lot about what is going on in a child's mind by looking in his or her eyes. If they look away from you when you ask them a question, then you know something is up. Make time to dine with your children.

- **There is a mother for all times.** I was never the "Macaroni Necklace Mom" and struggled through the early years. However, I hit my stride when my daughters got to middle school and became more verbal. I enjoy being the mother who takes the kids to concerts and has sleepovers. We all have different strengths, so don't feel inferior because you aren't excited to play with Silly Putty.

- **Keep things in perspective.** Most childhood memories begin around the age of six, so keep this in mind when you make a mistake. Don't beat yourself up over not having the right decorations for their birthday party, because they probably won't remember anyway.

- **Always have a back up plan.** I strongly recommend you develop a "back up plan" in case you get stuck at work and can't get away to do things like attend doctor appointments. Flexibility is key. Having a family member, friend, or babysitter willing to pitch in at the last minute can be invaluable.

- **Being a working mother is a humbling experience.** This is a harsh reality for many perfectionists who are used to getting everything right. Most working mothers will forget to pick their children up from something, whether day care or an after-school activity and miss or be late for a game or performance. Don't beat yourself up if this happens to you.

- **Children equal out by sixth grade.** Some children advance faster than others. Both of my children were late readers. In fact, my youngest has dyslexia. I remember hearing about other children reading Harry Potter in first grade, and my daughters were far below that level. They eventually became voracious readers once they found topics of interest. It is important for your child to be, at a minimum, on grade level. If you feel your child is struggling, talk to his or her teacher. My daughter's father and I were pleasantly surprised the first time we saw our oldest daughter's standardized test scores. I said, "Did you know she was this smart?" and his response was, "I had no clue."

Moving Forward While Raising Children

Having a child changes your perspective. You will be faced with a lot of hard choices, one of which is to slow down or temporarily stop your career. The other is how to move forward with the added responsibility. I can only tell you what worked for me: Compartmentalize and keep my home life at home and my business life at work. This will allow you to transition between one life and the other and focus on achieving goals. Many women use the time commuting between the office and home to prepare themselves for their other role. After you arrive at the office, you should make working your priority. The more you think about what is going on in your other world, the harder it is to focus on what is happening where you are. It is like stepping onto a court or field to play a big game. You push other thoughts out of your head and focus on the task at hand. Others around you will follow your lead. If you seem to be in control and professional, they might forget you just had a baby or are raising little kids and treat you the same as they did before you got pregnant. If it is not a big deal to you, it won't be to others.

However, you do need to pay attention to limitations. It is probably not wise to take on a promotion that requires a lot of travel or late-night work unless you have a partner who is willing to pick up the slack. These are things you must consider before making a decision to accept a promotion or a new job. *Do not expect any employer to change the rules for you.* By doing so, you ruin it for every other woman who comes after you.

CHAPTER 17

Balancing Work and Family

Establish Reasonable Expectations

As you progress in your career, make sure that you establish reasonable expectations for yourself. Look at the whole picture, including work, family, and professional development, as you are setting goals. I recently spoke to a young woman who had such high expectations for herself that she always felt as if she was falling short. After we talked, it became apparent that she had taken all her life goals and crammed them in to a 10-year timeline. I told her that she would have nothing to look forward to after the age of 40. This is especially true for women who are married and/or raising children. We want to do everything perfectly, even though we are juggling lots of balls in the air. Learn to cut yourself some slack and extend some of the time lines for goals.

Strive for a Balanced Life

You do not want to put all your eggs in one basket. When you have balance in each part of your life, it creates strength and harmony. For people who only have their job, their whole life is dependent on what happens at the office. This can be dangerous, because it can make you too reliant on your company. If something changes it can be devastating. You often see this when CEOs retire. Their social lives revolve around their jobs and after they quit, they lose their lifestyle. I have seen people go back to work just because they don't know what to do with themselves.

Maintaining a healthy lifestyle is also important. A nurse working in a hospital once told me that she has seen too many cases of people who have literally worked themselves sick. She tells them all that she has never heard someone say, while dying, that they wished they had spent more time at work.

Final Words of Wisdom

I was talking to someone the other evening, and he asked me how long I had been with my company. I said "25 years" and then showed him the ring I received as my service award. His response was that I had been married to my company for a long time, and he was glad they finally put a ring on my finger.

In my opinion, a successful career is like a good marriage: it is full of ups and downs. Sometimes you are crazy in love, and other times you can't stand them. This is natural because if there weren't bad times, you would not appreciate the good ones. Just as in a marriage, it takes a lot of hard work and commitment to make the relationship work.

If I can leave you with one more piece of advice, it is that life is a marathon, not a sprint to the finish line.

Most people will work for at least 40 years, so there is plenty of time to get things done. Find what makes you happy and then do it. I have provided you with some advice based on my life experiences to help you along your way. The rest is up to you. The most important thing to remember is that it is your life, and *if you love what you do, you can be successful!*

About the Author

Roseann Harrington, M.B.A.

With more than 25 years experience in marketing, communications, operations, and training, Roseann Harrington understands critical connections between word, image and message.

In her role as Vice President of Marketing, Communications & Community Relations with Orlando Utilities Commission, Harrington ensures OUC's nationally recognized brand, "The *Reliable* One."

Partnering with national and regional industry agencies, local government, media and community leaders, Harrington works to expand the reach of OUC's messages of conservation and a focus on the future of clean energy.

In addition to her work as a guest lecturer on corporate branding, leadership, building community outreach programs and gaining customer support, she has raised hundreds of thousands of dollars for area non-profit agencies through board work and donor event management.

In 2008, the Orlando Business Journal named Harrington one of Central Florida's Top 10 "Women Who Mean Business" for her successful corporate branding efforts at OUC. She has also received the Metropolitan Orlando Urban League's Dr. James R. Smith Award for outstanding humanitarianism and been named Downtowner of the Year by the Downtown Orlando Partnership for contributing to the growth of Orlando's central business district.

Harrington earned her bachelor's degree from Loyola University in New Orleans and a master's degree in business administration from the Crummer Graduate School of Business in Florida.